DA

Fac

THE COMMONWEALTH AND INTERNATIONAL LIBRARY
OF SCIENCE, TECHNOLOGY, ENGINEERING
AND LIBERAL STUDIES

Joint Chairmen of the Honorary Editorial Advisory Board

SIR ROBERT ROBINSON, o.m., f.r.s.
and DEAN ATHELSTAN SPILHAUS

Publisher
ROBERT MAXWELL, m.c.

MUSIC DIVISION

VOLUME 5

General Editor
K. A. WRIGHT

THE COMMON SENSE
OF SINGING

THE COMMON SENSE
OF SINGING

By

GEORGE BAKER

Hon.R.A.M., A.R.C.M.

Honorary Member of the Royal Philharmonic Society

PERGAMON PRESS

OXFORD · LONDON · PARIS · FRANKFURT

THE MACMILLAN COMPANY

NEW YORK

PERGAMON PRESS LTD.
Headington Hill Hall, Oxford
4 & 5 Fitzroy Square, London W.1

THE MACMILLAN COMPANY
60 Fifth Avenue, New York 11, New York

COLLIER-MACMILLAN CANADA, LTD.
132 Water Street South, Galt, Ontario, Canada

GAUTHIER-VILLARS ED.
55 Quai des Grands-Augustins, Paris 6

PERGAMON PRESS G.m.b.H.
Kaiserstrasse 75, Frankfurt am Main

Library of Congress Card No. 63-21131

Set in 11 on 12pt Bembo and printed in Great Britain by
PAGE BROS. (NORWICH) LTD.

CONTENTS

FOREWORD

BY

SIR ADRIAN C. BOULT, O.St.J.

M.A., D.Mus. Oxon., Hon. LL.D., etc.

——————wwwuվ/❽ၤทงงงง——————

GEORGE BAKER

WHERE artistic matters are concerned there is often a very delicate balance to be maintained between the tidiness of theory and the varied experiences of practice. I know how tempting it is slightly to distort an experience of fact in order to make it fit in with a pet theory which won't always hold water.

Readers can be assured that there is no danger in this book of even the slightest deviation from the straight path of the purest common sense, for Mr. George Baker has an enviable reputation on both sides of the art, having for many years been one of the most popular and respected singers in this country, who has, as well, never spared himself as a teacher, and has helped countless young artists on their way.

Those who discover that Mr. Baker's most recent Gilbert and Sullivan recordings were made for H.M.V. as recently as December 1962 will no doubt be surprised to know they bring his total to over 3000. They have embraced all kinds of music, from Opera to *Lieder*, and from Oratorio to 'pops', for he holds the view, which I consider is right, that "a working professional is one who is in the open market to be engaged to sing when and where required, and to perform to the best of his ability the work given to him to do" (Introduction). The astonishing fact to me is that all his recordings have been made continuously throughout a career extending over fifty-five years. That is a remarkable record for any singer and the best possible tribute to the soundness of his basic technique.

But that is only one side to his art. His musicianship is attested by academic diplomas won not only as a singer but also as an organist; and I know that his ability to learn and interpret unfamiliar (and often new) music quickly, coupled with unusual versatility, has greatly increased the demands for his services both here and in the New World. He lectures, examines and writes extensively; this book is a compendium of the wisdom and long experience of a man holding a unique position not merely in the world of singing, but in the greater world of Music itself.

I personally have the greatest pleasure in commending this book, for all British musicians are thinking now of the 150th birthday of the venerable Royal Philharmonic Society, and George Baker's name and mine are, I believe, two of the oldest now on the books of the Society. We joined as young enthusiasts almost on the same day, and Baker has given it most generously his time and energy in many capacities: member of Council, Treasurer, and now Chairman in this most notable year of its history.

INTRODUCTION

How MANY books have been written about the art, the science, the technique and the anatomy of singing? I do not know; probably the number runs into hundreds. However, I *do* know that I have more than a dozen on my library shelves and if, like the Colonel in W. S. Gilbert's "Patience", I (quoting freely)—

> "Took all these treaties all that are fusible,
> Melt them all down in a pipkin or crucible,
> Set them to simmer and take off the scum"—

what would the residuum be? An indigestible pudding of confusion and nonsense. The truth is, there are no commonly accepted principles of tutelage in the technique of singing. In no other field of education is there such chaos of ideas and opinions.

Nevertheless, there are in existence some excellent books on the subject and I am indebted to the authors of four of them, viz: *The Singing of the Future* by Ffrangcon-Davies (John Lane); *Dynamic Singing* by Louis Bachner (Dennis Dobson); *The Voice of the Mind* by E. Herbert-Caesari (Robert Hale); and *Interpretation in Song* by H. Plunket Greene (Macmillan & Co. and Stainer & Bell).

The preface to one of the less important books on singing in my possession starts with this sentence—"This book had to be written." A bold statement. I cannot convince myself that my book *had* to be written, because I hold to the opinion that the art of singing cannot be entirely learned from books, but I honestly feel that I have something of importance to say.

After 55 years of continuous employment as a professional singer and adjudicator, I do claim to know something about the human voice and how to use it. In putting my views, precepts and opinions before the reader I would like to state quite clearly that I address myself to ordinary people who like singing. I have always described myself as a working professional; that is, one who is in the open market to be engaged to sing when and where required, and to perform to the best of his ability the work given to him or her to do; and it is for the established and the embryo working professional, as well as lovers of singing generally, that this book is written. What I have to offer is the essence of a long experience as a public singer, an all-round musician[1], a musical administrator, an adjudicator and a teacher with a number of pupils who have achieved enviable success in life.

"What I have written, I have written" but, unlike Pontius Pilate who made this historic statement, not for the sake of political expediency but with an earnest desire to help, to clarify and if possible, to instruct.

There are no anatomical drawings in this book and I offer no apology for their absence, because whatever interest they may have for students of anatomy or as examples of drawing and design, they are of no help to anyone who wishes to understand and practice the art or the skill of singing. In short, this book purports to be a plain man's guide to the career of singing.

My grateful thanks are due to Miss Winifred Dodd for preparing the typescript of this book and for her invaluable help in checking the proofs. Also, I acknowledge with thanks the permission given to me to reproduce musical examples from (1) *Lulu* by Anton Berg by Universal Edition (Alfred A. Kalmus Ltd.) and (2) *Moses and Aaron* by Schönberg and *Elegy for Young Lovers* by Henze by Schott and Co. Ltd.

[1] A gossip column writer said of me, "He was once an organist."

TO MY WIFE
OLIVE GROVES

I

WHAT IS SINGING?

A CHALLENGING question indeed, whether one accents the first, the second or the third word of the query.

Since no two people seem to agree about what *is* singing I am reminded of the humorous monologue, "Sam, pick up th' musket", recited by that brilliant character-actor, Stanley Holloway. This monologue, written by the late Marriott Edgar, was about a fictitious Lancastrian soldier in the ranks of the Infantry who let his musket fall to the ground when the troops were lined up before the battle of Waterloo. Sam was annoyed by the accident, so much so that when ordered to pick up his musket he, with typical Lancastrian pugnacity, refused. The officers in ascending order of seniority pleaded with him to obey the order, but Sam still refused. Here was a dilemma and there was no time to spare. Eventually the great Duke of Wellington himself rode up and begged Sam, as a personal favour, to pick up his musket. Sam thought for a moment and then said, "Well—for *thee*, Duke—I'll pick it oop." Whereupon, the Duke, according to the loquacious Sam, thanked him and then gave the command, "Let battle commence."

1

When I drop the question, "What is Singing?" I certainly have a battle on my hands. So from now on it will be attack and strategic defence by turns, as any student of polemics well knows. The late Ernest Newman, a polemical critic if ever there was one, raised the question whether there *is* such a thing as singing; that is to say, singing *per se*. In the purely technical sense, of course, there is; singing means producing from the human throat or voice-box a succession of tones (sounds) at definite pitches and, so far as that definition is concerned, means producing sounds that are beautiful in themselves and in perfect tune with each other.

Even from this rudimentary point of view it is, I think, a fact that we seldom hear really good singing; or, to put it another way, we hear extremely little good singing in the purely technical sense of the term. There are good natural voices in plenty, and I make this statement without hesitation because I hear a hundred or so every year, and have done so for many years as a professional assessor, giving written reports on the potentialities of the candidates. This work must not be confused with adjudications at competitive musical festivals, which are amateur competitions and have little or nothing to do with the highly competitive professional market. Another factor in the state of the singer's art has been, and still is, the indifference, not to say hostility, towards fine singing on the part of a large percentage of our music critics. It is too much to expect that the critics should have the art and technique of every branch of musical activity at their finger-tips, but why singing should be the one branch they know least about is very puzzling, since they are called upon to occupy a considerable part of their time listening to and criticizing performances of opera and oratorio. I can think of only four music critics on the national Press in Great Britain whom I consider competent to give authoritative criticisms of singing. The rest are thoroughly honest and reputable critics, but the art, and particularly the technique of singing, for some inscrutable reason, seems to be a closed book to them. It is astonishing how they, the critics, will accept a singer producing any kind of sound which they would never tolerate from an instrumentalist. In fairness it could be said that the interpretation of certain operatic roles and occasional dramatic situations call for vocal sounds that are far removed from *bel canto*, but these are exceptional cases. Dramatic truth is at all times a prerequisite of art but *verismo* which leads to vocal suicide should never be tolerated.

It may be that we have been listening to second-rate singing for so long that we all fail to realize how far from the first-rate seventy-five per cent of even the best singing is. It is one of my professional commitments to listen, as a critic, to a large number of radio performances, including broadcasts from Bayreuth and other opera houses both at home and abroad. The radio being a non-visual medium, there is nothing to attract my attention but what I actually hear. What have I heard? In Wagner operas a welter of glorious orchestral sound, through which floated radiant sopranos; struggling, flat-singing tenors; sonorous basses without any low notes and baritones who shout. On the whole, a disappointing sound-picture, and one is not surprised that the critics devote all their attention to assessing the losses or gains in Wieland or Wolfgang Wagner's production and stage picture. I have heard performances of some of Verdi's masterpieces from other opera houses, when the "stars" (some of them) have given such dazzling performances that one was compelled to liken them to electric eels trying to evade capture by the conductor. It was all very exciting.

Then again, I have heard innumerable recitals by intellectual singers, those who possess everything but an instrument on which to perform; in other words, minus a voice. As non-visual performances they are meagre fare indeed. It is a rarity to turn on the radio and to be able to say truthfully, "What a beautiful voice and what a well-sustained vocal line." It may be that the possessor of the beautiful voice has little else to offer, but that is a deficiency which even the most casual listener will quickly discover for him- or herself. Never forget that Mr. & Mrs. Everybody—and they constitute the world's audience—seldom make a mistake as to who is a singer and who is not. They may thoughtlessly enjoy the flesh-pot of a lovely voice unaccompanied, as is sometimes the case, by any trace of brains or sense of poetry, but when the complete artist appears they recognize him at once. Voice is not everything. That remark has been made so often it has become a cliché; nevertheless it is true. If we accept it as a truth, is it not also true that musical intelligence alone is not sufficient to make a singer? To become a singer it is necessary to have a voice and a lot of other things, too, but first of all a voice.

What some people call a voice I call a noise, so let me give my definition of a *voice*. A voice is the sound that is created by exhaling a column of breath which is set in vibration by its impact with the vocal cords and afterwards increased in volume by the various resonators through which it passes.

The resonators are in the mask. They are the spaces bounded by the teeth, palates, the face and the sinuses in the front of the face and head. In opposition to all the writers on singing who have devoted chapters to the resonators and how to find them and use them, I assert that written instructions are valueless to students of singing. Practical tuition plus the use of one's own ears is the only way to learn how to acquire the automatic use of the various resonators nature has provided. I will go further, and in company with Louis Bachner, say that one cannot develop resonance *per se*.

The primary vibrations produced by the action of the breath on the vocal cords causes the air in the resonance chamber or cavities to vibrate and thus creates resonance. The freer the primary vibrations the greater the intensity of the resonance.

I cannot at this point start a subsidiary battle with the Sinus Tone Production school of thought and I do not intend to do so, because I believe that we sing with the throat, not over the throat or in the sinuses. The value of the vocal cords in sound production is not in my considered opinion a legend, but a fact. Anyone who has had the painful experience of hearing people try to speak who have undergone an operation for the removal of cancer in the larynx cannot have any doubt about the primary generation of sound as it relates to either speech or song which, I maintain, are *almost* one and the same thing.

But let me return to my definition of a voice. The sound, i.e., the voice that is emitted and projected into the air, must have at least some sensuous quality, or in plainer language, it should fall easily on the ear. A sensitive musical ear will always recoil from a vocal noise that is, for instance, metallic or goat-like in quality.

Therefore my first requirement of one who wishes to become a singer is that he or she must possess a voice. As singing is a combination of voice, technique, magnetism (or personality), a sense of truth and beauty and a command of tone colour, it necessarily follows that the fortunate possessor of all these attributes, acquired or inborn, is in every sense of the word a good singer. As our goal is good singing, let us consider what is the basis of it.

To sing well four things or conditions are essential:

1. Clear articulation.
2. Easy and natural breathing.
3. The ability to tie the articulations one to the other in sustaining the voice—in other words, a perfect technique.
4. Mental control of tone colour.

There is one other condition, not absolutely essential, but most desirable, and that is personal magnetism. This, however, is a pure gift and I fear can never be acquired.

Clear articulation is the basis of all singing and holds in itself all the study of singing, if we couple with it the emotional timbre and the joining of the words in sustaining the sound. Plunket Greene described this succinctly as "Sing as you speak." Ffrangcon-Davies with equal succinctness said "Singing is a sustained talking on a tune." Some may say correctness of intonation is the basis of singing and must be the first demand. This is true, but I regard it as a minimum to be exacted from all musicians. It is not *ipso facto* an artistic quality of singing, whereas articulation is the basis of all artistic singing. Coquelin (the great French actor) says: "It is at the same time the ABC and the highest point of art. One must learn it in the beginning as children learn civility." When one addresses oneself to the public one must make oneself understood and therefore it is essential to articulate distinctly.

One sings to *express* and that can only be done through the words. There is no doubt that one cannot sing without a voice, but the voice itself does not suffice in lyrical diction; it can often be almost a handicap. Voice and brains are not synonymous terms. If a singer with a magnificent voice cannot articulate properly the sound will smother the words and the vowels will hide the consonants. In short, the singer sets up such a noise (good though it be) that he is often scarcely intelligible. The most beautiful song finds itself transformed into a vocal exercise, no longer expresses any idea, and loses all its charm. On the other hand, such is the power of perfect articulation that it can make us forget the shortcomings of the voice and will allow the least endowed of singers to make himself both heard and understood. "Talk on a tune" and you will get at the hearts of the audience. A singer who cannot get at the hearts or brains of an audience *has* no audience, and a singer without an audience is as one struck dumb.

It has always seemed very odd to me that people throughout the world who use English as their day-to-day language care so little about it, and for the most part have never learned how to pronounce it. The late George Bernard Shaw (an Irishman) made a trenchant observation in his Preface to *Pygmalion*, "The English have no respect for their language, and will not teach their children to speak it. . . it is impossible for an Englishman to open his mouth without making some other Englishman despise him." This was, of course, a shaft of wit aimed at the snob value some people attach to certain so-called cultured dialects. The following examples will explain what I mean:

    nation—netion (to rhyme with session)
    world—wairld
    first—fairst

work—wairk
same—sem
opera—opprah
o—it is impossible to give a phonetic illustration of the pinched
sound adopted by professedly cultured people.
ah—the modern tendency is to pronounce it with the widest
possible opening of the mouth; the Australian sound of "ah",
not the Italian pure vowel "ah".

The trouble is that the English language as spoken in various
parts of the world has more dialects than any other language under
the sun. I have no objection to dialects as such—they lend colour
to the language; indeed, I have no doubt that we all could be
accused of having traces of some sort of dialect in our daily speech;
my own is basically Merseyside, and that, not to mince matters,
is a corrupt form of Irish.

I am used to dialects, having travelled as a working professional
over a large part of the world. I have sung and acted in over
eighty-five towns in the U.S.A., and played with American
actors; I have sung and acted in Australia, and have toured in
Canada and South Africa. Now the point I wish to make is that
in the theatre or on the concert platform all the performers with
whom I have been associated have spoken and sung in public with
a standard pronunciation that could be immediately understood
and was intelligible to English-speaking audiences anywhere,
unless of course they were comedians or character actors. Perhaps
the best example of standard English is that employed in performances of Shakespeare. Dialects refined or unrefined in Shakespeare
are only acceptable in character rôles.

The question now arises, what is the standard English pronunciation? The common denominator must surely be English
spoken with free and pure vowels. Another question: Are the
English vowels pure? Some singing teachers say they are not.

Instead of quoting the edicts of masters of singing of that period
known as the Golden Age of Song, let me quote a much-admired

singer nearer our own time, namely, Benjamino Gigli. He said,
"The so-called Italian vowels A, E, I, O, U (the five vowels as
conceived and pronounced by the Italians) constitute the true
basis of voice and song, that is, of the Bel Canto."[1] Italian singers
speak as they sing because they express themselves for the most
part with the aforesaid five pure vowels.

The use of these pure or monophthongal vowels are often subject
to modifications for purposes of coloration or for vocal adjustment as one ascends a scale—but that need not concern us at
the moment. The point we have to consider is, are the English
vowels diphthongal? The Italians would say yes, and strictly
speaking some of them are; but we are not Italians, and when *we*
say "oh" we conclude the operation of saying it by bringing the
lips together producing this sound: "oh-oo". The Italian vowel
"oh" is an open "o" sound suspended in mid-air, without a
terminal.

I cannot hear any difference between the Italian "ah" and the
English "ah"; to my ear they are the same sound. It is true I have
heard singers saying "ah-ee" but that is merely bad enunciation.

The English "eh" vowel (Italian "e") is, like the "oh", diphthongal—"eh-ee".

For the sake of clarity, let me set out the vowels as English-
speaking people see them, hear them and say them:

$$a—eh-ee$$
$$e—ee$$
$$i—i-ee$$
$$o—o-oo$$
$$oo—oo$$

To these must be added the "ah" which is common to nearly all
languages.

---

[1] *The Voice of the Mind* by E. Herbert-Caesari.

The Italian vowels are:

a—ah
e—eh as in "May" without the terminal
i—ee as in "eel"
o—o as in the first syllable of "motive"
oo—oo as in English

With these two tables before us we have a pretty good working guide to the mastery of pure vowel sounds in the basically vowel language of the Italians and the diphthongal variations of the English language. The variations will be very slight indeed if one acquires the habit of speaking English clearly and without social and local affectations.

Faulty production and impure vowel sounds are interlocked. It has often been said that English is not a good language in which to sing. This I emphatically deny. The English language correctly spoken or sung is capable of great expression and varieties of colour. Believing as I do that it is possible to sing as you speak, and mark, with *all* the subtle inflexions of speech, it behoves us to pronounce our language in the right way; that is, with pure vowel sounds. To achieve this the vowel must be mentally conceived as a true sound and then articulated with the mouth and lips in the shape of the vowel. For example, think of "o" as a round sound and sing it with an o-shaped mouth. The "i" in "wide" must have a wide mouth or the vowel loses its character and meaning. "A" (pronounced "ey") and "e" should have an elbow-touching relationship. The "a" vowel should be given a little more space than "e". If the jaw is allowed to drop or sag when singing the vowel "e" the sound merges into "a". If the "a" vowel is given more than its normal space the sound merges into something like "er". There are of course occasions when modifications are made in order to cover the voice for high notes or for special emotional reasons, but these are the fundamental principles.

I have just said that faulty production and impure vowel sounds are interlocked. Most people will agree with this statement, but will follow on with the question of how to cure a throaty singer merely by making him sing vowels or complete words. The answer is simple. If a pupil sings or attempts to sing "ah" with a throaty production (i.e., a tight throat) he is *not* singing "ah", he is merely making a noise. Make him *say* "ah", not mumble it, but speak it as if addressing an audience, then find the musical note corresponding to the pitch of his ordinary speaking voice. He should then be made to speak and sing "ah" alternately in rapid succession until his ear accustoms itself to the new sensation of a clear open tone. In passing I may say that I have found this method almost fool-proof in dealing with clergymen and priests who have tied themselves up in vocal knots trying to sing plain-song (or what they imagine is singing) instead of speaking the words on the simple tune that plainsong is, and at a pitch that is as close as possible to their speaking voices when being used to address a concourse of people—not the normal conversational mumble. The vowel "ah" spoken and sung must on no account be the sound that one hears so often in the society of people generally accepted as upper class. The common variety with a wide mouth is the one to ensure an open throat. In all stages of singing it is essential that there should not be any stiffening of the body, and it is the teacher's task to see that his pupils do not stiffen their minds. In other words, a mental state of happy confidence will break down the self-consciousness and doubt that gives birth to so many adult vocal troubles. I say *adult*, because children are not afflicted in this way. Without relaxation the vocal chords cannot work properly.

It is most important that the student should hear the difference between the good and the bad in his own singing.

A singer may know all about the throat, nose and ear from the physiological point of view—but the knowledge will be entirely useless unless he can train his ear to appreciate the difference between right and wrong.

Speaking and singing are learned by ear. If you tell a Cockney that the word is "railway" not "rileway", or an American that the name of an east-coast seaside resort is "Atlantic City" not "Aclannic Sirry" or an Australian that the capital of New South Wales is "Sydney" not "Sidnee" or a South African that the man who works on the land is a "farmer" not a "former", not only will they wonder what you are getting at but they will all roundly declare that to the best of their belief they have pronounced the words correctly. Until the pupil can *hear* the difference in the pronunciation it is hopeless to expect a change.

At this stage it may occur to the reader that I have not, so far, made any mention of scales and exercises. As these are merely adjuncts to the acquisition of vocal freedom I shall take up the matter in the chapter on technique.

The first essential condition that I have laid down for singing is clear articulation. I emphasize that the generating factor in singing is the mental desire and urge to do so. Clear articulation can only be achieved by acquiring the same vocal freedom in song as in speech. When one talks, the body is relaxed and the mind holds sway. Relaxation of the body is dependent on the mind, therefore think happiness and contentment and the vocal muscles will relax in answer to your mental state and be free to work naturally. The more freedom a singer acquires the more surely will his individuality reveal itself. Freedom is the fundamental basis of all singing. As in acting and public-speaking, the personal element is of very great importance. Whether one likes it or not, the solo performer is supreme and must be supreme in the public arena. It behoves us therefore to make our appearance before the public as attractive and compelling as possible. The singer's power of attraction lies in the truth of expression that he gives to words and the thoughts behind them. This is achieved in a mechanical way by free and clear articulation, and in a spiritual way by the controlling force of a poetic mind and a just will.

I well remember Adele and Fred Astaire when they first came to London and by their virility, professional expertise, charm and personal magnetism had all the lovers of the theatre worshipping at their feet. They sang a song with the intriguing and bewildering title,

"The which-ness of the what-ness and the where-ness of the who."
The which, the what and the where may remain for ever a matter
for speculative thought, but as the singing instrument is a living
thing, a part of the human body, the "who" is a known factor. It
is you, me, everybody who has the desire and the will to sing.

II

BREATHING

All that has life and breath,
Sing to the Lord
            Hymn of Praise—*Mendelssohn.*

SINCE there can be no life without breath the subject of breathing is one of great importance to us all, and for singers it has a supreme importance. With a somewhat pedantic regard for the literal truth a well-known writer has declared that, so far as singing is concerned, breathing is only a means to an end. I cannot wholly accept this, because the statement tends to minimize the importance of breathing. Without easy and natural breathing, free and untrammelled singing is impossible.

There has been a lot of nonsense written by faddists and charlatans about breathing, resulting in a shrouding of the subject with an air of inscrutable mystery.

The object in taking a breath is not to store it up in the chest, but to let it out again in a steady controlled flow; but there must be no waste of breath or gusty escape. Any attempt to hold the breath back leads inevitably to muscular stiffness, and this is the death-blow to all singing. Nature has ordained that in order to live we must breathe, and it is certainly not arguable that this natural and auto-matic human function should be one of difficulty. Normally one

13

does not experience any trouble in breathing for the purposes of walking or talking, but breathing in singing requires special training and development. My theory about breathing is so simple that it may have the same effect on the reader as the prophet's simple advice had on Naaman who consulted him about a cure for his illness— send him away in a rage!

The action of breathing is upwards—from the bottom to the top. I might almost say from the feet upwards. This remark is not quite as absurd as it may sound. It should not be forgotten that the whole muscular system is brought into play in singing.

Breathing is the process of inhaling and exhaling the air. The lungs contain the air without which no sound can be formed. They admit it through the mouth, the nostrils, the pharynx, the glottis and the trachea, and expel it again through the same channels. The lungs are contained in the chest cavity and have for their base the diaphragm. The diaphragm is a large muscle, closing the cavity between the ribs, and forms the floor of the chest, separating the chest (or thorax) from the abdomen. In repose its shape is dome-like. The moment the breath enters the body the diaphragm flattens, the upper abdomen protrudes slightly, and as the act of inhalation continues the walls of the chest (the ribs) expand all round and the upper abdomen *contracts*. The lungs, having gradually filled, should expand from back to front and from top to bottom.

Let me state the movements more clearly.

The first thing to establish is the correct posture or stance. Stand erect with the weight of the body on the ball of the foot, pull in the buttocks and, as it were, tuck them under. At the same time, in one co-ordinated action, draw in the abdomen—draw it *in* and *up*. Next, inhale through the mouth or nose, or both; the breath enters the lungs causing them to expand. The lungs, let me repeat, are in the chest cavity, they are not in the stomach or abdomen. As the lungs expand through the intake of breath the chest walls also expand, and the chest itself should be lifted up and out. All the muscular activity that controls the act of breathing takes place principally in the chest and all the muscles act automatically as the lungs distend.

At this point let me emphasize that the diaphragm also acts automatically and has done so from the time when, as new-born babies, we drew our first breath. Diaphragmatic breathing or the attempted conscious control of the diaphragm is not only wrong but dangerous, because it causes muscular rigidity, and that in itself is the enemy of flexibility and freedom. To breathe freely it is necessary that the chest should be in a correct position—up and out, and the shoulders back. Never forget that all the component parts of the breathing apparatus act automatically (if correctly used) because the lungs fill with air. There are no other fancy reasons. Furthermore, and this is very important, there must be no preparatory or anticipatory tensions of any sort whatsoever before inhalation. Conscious control of any muscular activity is a fundamental error in all singing. To sum up the precepts so far expounded, let me express myself in simple terms: when you commence to sing forget all about the diaphragm and the rest of the breathing machinery; sing on the air that should be, in sensation, under the larynx.

Deep breathing has no anatomical application; it simply means, a full breath. Do let us get this one cardinal fact into our heads; there are no lungs in the abdomen, therefore one cannot breathe there; *but* the abdominal muscles must retain their in-and-up firmness throughout the act of breathing and singing.

A steady and even outflow of breath is purely a question of will-power. The breathing apparatus must obey the singer's will—but it is most important that the student should not ask his respiratory organs to work beyond their capacity. In other words—do not try to inflate yourself like a football. Take a comfortable breath and at the same time give your chest the biggest expansion possible, always remembering not to stiffen the body or tighten the muscles.

Having taken your breath in, let it flow out; not just anyhow, but in order to make and support the sounds (the words) you have willed. I will say it again. Take a breath—having taken it *let it flow out*!

Before I conclude this chapter on breathing, may I offer these warnings: (1) Let there be no forcing of the breath against the vocal cords. (2) Never stiffen the diaphragm before the act of singing in order to (what is called) "support the tone." A stiff diaphragm does not support the tone; it only stiffens it and eventually destroys it. (3) Methods of singing, the aim of which is to control breathing by muscular action or actions, are basically wrong. (4) Do not be misled into thinking that one's ability to juggle with names like Thorax, Trachea, Glottis, Pharynx, or to know that the diaphragm in a state of repose is the shape of a dome, will help one to breathe or sing any better. It is useful knowledge about the anatomy of singing but it has nothing whatever to do with the art of singing.

Sir Charles Santley who, with Battistini, was one of the greatest baritones of all time, said, with characteristic bluntness, on the only occasion upon which I met him and talked with him, "Show me the man who knows all about the larynx and the glottis and I'll show you a man who can't sing."

Breathing is simply and purely a natural physical function which can be developed through breathing exercises, but useful though these are they should be undertaken only under the guidance of a competent teacher. The following suggestions may be a help to students. First, take up the correct stance, as already described. Next, take a full but comfortable breath. Now (1) exhale on a humming sound with closed lips; (2) exhale on a hum with loose lips. If the breath flows at an even pressure it should cause the lips to vibrate a little. (3) Exhale on the consonant S, the tongue resting lightly on the upper and forward part of the palate. As in (1) and (2) there must be no conscious control of the breath other than the steadiness of its outward flow—leaving the throat completely free.

It will be noticed that the points of resistance are in the nose, the lips and in the mouth in that order; but all three exercises bring the focal point to the front of the mouth, i.e., the lips, and bring us back to my fundamental contention that clear articulation and a free-flowing breath is the basis of all singing. The truth is, the best breathing exercise of all is singing itself.

So, once again I say, take a breath, and having taken it, let it flow out, and your song will take wing.

III

ARTICULATION AND
TONE-COLOUR

THESE two essential conditions which, in Chapter I, I described, with two other conditions, as the basis of good singing and referred to as numbers 3 and 4, are to a large extent interlocked; therefore I shall treat them in dissertation as a composer might treat two closely-related themes.

If we accept the premise that singing is a sustained talking on a tune we must learn how to tie the articulations one to the other in sustaining the voice.

Also, in order to give meaning to what we have to say, we shall have to acquire the art and the skill of colouring the tones or the sounds we produce. But first things first.

To tie the articulations one to the other to create a sustained vocal line is not at the outset very easy. Nevertheless, it *can* be learned by any normally intelligent person with musical and poetic feeling and a sense of melodic flow. It is what is usually called *legato* singing, and is a rarer accomplishment than one would imagine. Students spend months singing slow exercises in order to perfect their legato singing, and then fail because they do not understand what *legato* means,

Legato means "connected"; that is, the sound of each note of a phrase being sustained until the next is heard. In singing, each *word* or syllable is sustained until the next is heard. You may think that if one ties the articulations one to the other an incomprehensible jumble of phonetic sounds will result or, again, the words will run one into the other. So they will, because we intend them to do so, but each word or syllable will be complete in itself and absolutely clear if articulated and sustained in the right way. The rule is to hold the vowel sound of the word to the fullest time limit of the musical note, and not to sing the next word until the precise time arrives for it to be sung—on no account must there be any interruption.

Take these words: "Let me go."

This is how it should be sung—"Le-tme-go":

   not like this—"Let, me, go":

   or worse still—"Let-ter-me-go".

  Another example:

   the wrong way—"Man-er of God":

   the right way—"Ma-nof-God".

The singer must take particular care to sing through the consonant "n" in the word "man", otherwise it may sound something like this—

   "Ma-nnof God"—

which is a gross exaggeration of what I mean and would be manifestly absurd.

Then there is the joining of words that end with the same consonant as the next word starts with:

Example: "Hide dawn from my sleepy eyes."

This is the non-*legato* and the usual way it would be sung—

   "Hi-der-dawn fro-mer-my sleepy eyes".

This is not done so much through slovenliness as through a wrong-headed desire to sound separately both the "d" in "Hide" and the "d" in "dawn", and also the "m" in "from" and "my". If you speak this line you will realize that you are attempting the impossible; that is to say if you still wish the words to sound like English. This is the way it should be sung:

   "Hi-ddawn fro-mmy".

The "dd" and "mm" represent the extra emphasis of the consonant required. The words "sleepy eyes" are not slurred thus—sleepy-yeyes—they join naturally, but yet remain distinct, because "eyes" starts with a vowel, and words commencing with a vowel should always have a clean and separate attack as in the German language.

To put it another way, give the vowel sound almost more than full value, snap in the final consonant (if any) and the next word appears instantly. Each word must be perfectly conceived and executed and yet you should not be able to put a piece of cigarette paper between any of them. To obtain this result one needs great mental concentration, a loose jaw, and the tongue and lips must work with the slickness of a machine.

I maintain that the principles of clear articulation are to a great extent the same in both speaking and singing, but it must be borne in mind that articulation in singing requires finer shades of development and shaping because the compass or range of pitch is more extensive and there are, at all times, specific musical demands. Some people have a naturally free and clear articulation, others—a minority, I believe—have speech defects of various kinds such as lisps, adenoidal troubles and stammers. It might be apposite and helpful if I instanced myself as one who had speech troubles in childhood and youth. I was a stammerer up to the age of sixteen or seventeen but with my father's help and encouragement I was able gradually to conquer the defect and through sheer necessity evolved a curative mechanism that in time became automatic. My father—a singer himself—was fond of quoting William Byrd (1538–1628) who said, in recommending the practice of singing, that it was a cure for stammerers.[1] Never were truer words uttered. It is an indisputable fact that it is *impossible* to stammer when singing, the reason being that the constantly changing pitches of sound prevent the articulatory apparatus from "stalling" or "seizing up".

I have already said that one should "sing as you speak", therefore the obvious corollary to this statement as applied to those with

[1] "It is a singular good remedie for a stutting and stammering in the speech."

speech defects is "speak as you sing". In other words, use a wider range of pitch and at all costs relax and let the breath flow out. That it can be done I, of all people, know. It is highly probable that because I had, as I have already said, through sheer necessity to take special and particular care in articulation when a youth, that in later life I became one of the best-known singers of the Gilbert and Sullivan patter songs. My many H.M.V. records are a proof of this somewhat egotistical statement.

But to return to normal cases and to the question of articulation in singing. As I have already said in Chapter I there are five fundamental or primary vowel sounds, but vowels have modifications in speech, and certainly there are modifications in singing dictated by the pitch of the sound. Consonants—lingual, explosive, palatal, sibilant—and their combinations collectively make up all the other forms of articulation. The vowel "i" (the Italian "ee") or "e" (in English) causes the closest or narrowest complete approximation of the vocal cords. Because it brings, in fact and by physical sensation, the cords together, singers have been notable for their habit of walking about dressing-rooms singing "mee-mee-mee-mee" in an attempt to, as it were, put an edge on the sounds they propose to make. It is not of itself a good habit, and does not necessarily make for freedom in singing. A long, sustained exhalation of the "ah", or, better still, a long exhalation of breath on a joined "ah-ey-ee" would be more helpful, because these vowels produce an intensity of tone.

The vowels "o" and "oo" are spoken of as "open" vowels, and "o" definitely is so in sensation and sound, but "oo" is only open because it has little intensity; indeed so little that when used in singing forte or mezzo-forte one has to use the vowel in a modified or what the shorthand writers would call a short vowel form. In *this* form it is absolutely necessary for the singer to protrude the lips as far as possible in order to retain the flavour of the vowel sound. Our ears have been assailed for years with loud-voiced baritones singing (in Sullivan's opera *Patience*) about a "Heavy Dragøne" instead of "Dragoon". Operatic baritones are generally the worst offenders.

Vowels are modified or rounded as the pitch ascends, but the modifications are so gradual and, one might say, infinitesimal, that the vocal adjustments take place automatically. There should never be any conscious control in spite of what the "voice-placers" may say. Since the human voice is not a portable instrument, one cannot take hold of it and place it anywhere. The term "placing the voice" is, I agree, one in common use; indeed it has almost a traditional use, but it can be misunderstood and lead to results that are undesirable. All such terms or directions are really valid attempts to describe physical sensations that are an integral part of free and untrammelled voice production.

Articulation and tone work hand-in-hand and the control of the vowel adjustments are brought about simply and solely by the mental and aural concentrations on the intensity of the tone you wish and will to make. In articulation, the lips and the tongue should at all times be completely free to meet all the demands made of them. The demands in comic opera and classical *Dramma Buffa* are often very considerable. Here is an example from *Don Pasquale* by Donizetti, Act III, Scene V:

C

and so on. The whole passage consists of eight bars of patter on one note, with recurrences during the Scene.

As a preparation for this and similar syllabic feats, learn and practice singing the Major-General's Song in Act I of *The Pirates of Penzance* by Sullivan:

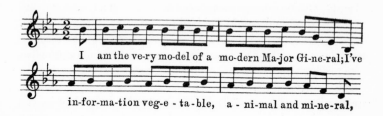

If you succeed in singing this difficult song with machine-like accuracy—words, notes and rhythm—at a rapid pace and at the same time give *meaning* to the words you will be ready to face any patter songs you may be called upon to sing in the normal operatic repertoire of *Opera Buffa*. It is absolutely essential in patter singing, as it is in vocal *fioritura* to take the weight off the voice; and lastly, do be warned that the mere tapping out of syllables with the precision of a typewriter results in nothing more than senseless jabbering.

It is sad to reflect that the art of genuine *buffo* singing has few practitioners in our generation. The elephantine vocal gambols of most of the contemporary *buffo* singers are a poor substitute for the lingual pyrotechnics of the singers of a past era to whom the words *bel canto* had a functional meaning.

Meaning—yes, that is the operative word, and the one that links articulation with both the meaning and tone-colour of words and the sound of words.

All emotion, all spontaneous sentiment, betrays itself in our faces; in our eyes, our cheeks, our lips and of course in the sound of our voices. But all these evidences of emotion are only the outward and visible signs of the inward workings of our minds. It follows, therefore, that tone-colour must be controlled, first and last, by the mind.

We mentally grasp and absorb the emotional content of a song, and then by force of will convey the mental picture to our hearers in its true colours. In singing, the inflexion is fixed by the melody. In other words, the melodic curve is fixed by the composer, as well as the key, the time and the rhythm. It is left to the singer to add the exact vocal expression.

If the singer is content to reclothe this music in a personal sound, however beautiful, and to add only the ordinary marks of musical expression, we may be able to distinguish the passion, the dramatic accents or the noble gestures, but it is doubtful if we shall know whether it is a question of love or hate, of joy or sorrow.

This music reclothed in sound may please or astonish us, but it will engender no emotion, because the song is lacking in expression, has no variety of colour or emotional atmosphere.

How does one obtain this emotional timbre or colouring of the voice? The mechanism is simple. Think the sound you wish to produce—cheerful, sad, angry, tender, and so on—and then translate your thoughts by means of the free play of the facial muscles, what the French call *la physionomie plastique*. The emotional mechanism is at once mental and mimic. To translate an emotional thought a good singer avails himself of both parts of the machine, mental and mimic, and the adjustment between these parts must always be absolute and complete, for by nature (mother nature) they are indissolubly tied. *Human* nature, however, frequently divorces them, as long-suffering and patient audiences are well aware. The words must not only mean what they say, but sound what they mean.

Here is an elementary instance:

The word "bright" is conceived in the mind *as* something bright, but unless translated by the bright play of the features its meaning is lost and the resultant vocal tone will be false. I am not exaggerating when I say that I have often heard the word "gay" sung with a sad mouth and face and a tone as gloomy as a funeral.

Another reason for the absence of true tone-colour is the singer's preoccupation with his own personal ideas of what is a good sound. A vocal tone that has no relation to the word sung never sounds good to me. It is just a noise, although I readily admit that it is some-times a very pleasant one.

This preoccupation with sound is a serious fault with most singers. If they would only remember that singing and speech are as one they would at long last realize that there is no tone that is not at once a word or a syllable. The greatest vocal results can only be obtained by a natural and fundamentally correct technique. Now the "natural" is not—as is generally supposed—a gift of nature. It is acquired, often with difficulty—hence my reference to a correct technique. The process of acquiring it is of itself the building up of a technique.

How is it that the exclamation "Ah!" can express so many varieties of meaning? It is because the emotional meaning is not so much in the word itself as in the tone-colour and the pitch used in singing it, this tone-colour being dictated by the mental picture in the brain.

Fugère, a great French baritone of a previous generation and at one time the grand old man of the Opera Comique, said: "the timbre emotional ought to be at the base of the vocal mechanism" and "the emotional mechanism is the only true mechanism of singing." Inasmuch as all human actions and reactions are born in the mind and controlled by the mind, I agree. But he goes on to say that "all singing exercises ought to be executed with a certain coloration of the sound." However, with this advice I do not agree. It seems to me impossible to correct faults if we do not insist, at all events in the elementary stages, on absolute purity of vowel sounds. The coloration of the sound must come at a later stage in the singer's training, when we can be certain that the student has rid himself of all the vocal shackles to which human nature is heir.

It has been said "the voice is not one instrument, it is a collection of instruments of varying timbres, in fact a veritable vocal orchestra." The point is a good one, but the word "orchestra" rather overstates the case. I would compare the voice to a stringed instrument, and by this I mean a stringed instrument with at least three strings, not a one-stringed fiddle! Unhappily, most of the singing one hears reminds one of the one-stringed fiddle. This is brought about by the cursed preoccupation with what is called "tone". The approach to singing should be through a mental and aural picture of drawing the bow across the strings. In a phrase, singing is string-playing, not tap-dancing. The violinist who can only play in the first position is not considered a player; why then should a singer who only sings in one tone-quality be regarded as anything but a bore or a duffer?

All voices have various strings to play on, but the difference in the tone of the strings is less distinguishable in the soprano voice than in any of the others. The soprano who can use the various strings in the voice instead of singing like a choir-boy or emulating a steam whistle is much to be envied, and has a great deal to be proud of. Alas, there are few, and it is possibly because of this scarcity that Maria Callas and Victoria de los Angeles have been acclaimed by audiences everywhere as the wonderfully emotional singers they are. When heart speaks to heart the ifs and the buts of the musical anatomists can be thrown away.

As an example of what I mean by using the three strings or resonators in the human voice let us examine a solo for the baritone voice from Mendelssohn's *Elijah*, "For the mountains shall depart", a straight-forward lyrical and *legato* tune. The three strings or resonators are upper, middle and lower, and I number them respectively, 1, 2 and 3.

It must be clearly understood that I am not talking about "registers" as that term is normally understood, or more often misunderstood.

Registers, which could aptly be described as resonating platforms, are subtle adjustments of the vocal apparatus governed by changes of pitch and which in a truly free production take place automatically. What is required is constant intensity or concentration of tone, supported by a steady out-flow of breath and without regard to the *volume* of tone. In speaking of "strings" I am referring to vocal colour or tone-quality.

Now let us proceed with the song:

2
For the mountains shall depart
2
and the hills, the hills be removed
2
but Thy kindness shall not depart
2   1
but Thy kindness, Thy kindness shall not
1   2
depart from me neither shall the covenant
2
of Thy peace of Thy peace be removed
1
neither shall the covenant of Thy peace be
1   2
removed but Thy kindness shall not depart
2
shall not depart but Thy kindness shall
2
not depart, shall not depart from me
3   1
neither shall be removed the covenant
1
of Thy peace

It will be noticed that the word "removed" finishes on a low B natural, and although the following word "the" is on the same note, it must be sung with the quality of the upper voice. It must never be assumed that because a musical phrase descends the quality must necessarily take on a heavier or more bass-like character.

Another instance of the use made of the various "strings" in the voice is an octave passage in the "Flower Song" from Bizet's *Carmen* (Act II) near the end of the song—"*Et j'étais une chose a toi*". The phrase starts on middle B flat and ascends to a high B flat. Never make the mistake of commencing it on a middle quality or stretching it by sheer force up to the high note. It is my contention that the entire phrase should be sung on the number 1 string.

With these theories in mind I recommend as a study "Toddesehn-sucht" or " 'Twas in the cool of eventide" by Bach.

If singers would really mean what they say, and make what is said sound what it means, they would experience little difficulty in mastering the art of colouring the voice. Let the emotions expressed show in the face; in short, act with the face. This is the secret of Fischer-Dieskau's hold on the public. He has a good and attractive voice, but that in itself is not sufficient to capture the public in the way he has done. Personality he has in abundance, but in the case of Fischer-Dieskau his voice *is* his personality. He acts with his voice, and the man or woman who can do that never lacks an audience. There is a school of musical humbugs who despise singers who act with their faces or voices; they refer to it as "mere performing." Well, they are right, it *is* performing, and so it should be. Always remember that a singer is just as much a performer as an acrobat, a politician, a barrister, a jockey or a professional beggar.

> "All the world's a stage
> And all the men and women merely players."

In these days when the world of entertainment is dominated by motion pictures and TV, one is accustomed to the word "projection", so let me sum up this chapter by saying *project the mind through the word*. A cultured mind will beget a cultured pronunciation, and this in its turn will beget a fine and right tone, i.e., the right tone-colour.

IV

TECHNIQUE

THE PRECEPTS which have so far been expounded in the foregoing chapters are all integral parts of the technique of singing; all that can now be included in a chapter specifically headed "Technique" will be hints, suggestions and definite rules as to how facility can be obtained in the use and the application of the fundamental laws of technique. This is a highly contentious subject and the welter of arguments, disputes and illogical ideas have brought about the chaos of opinions to which I referred in the Introduction to this book. I have actually met and known people who have openly declared that they have never bothered their heads about technique and had no intention of doing so. "If you have a voice", they say, "use it; and if you have anything in your mind to which you wish to give expression, give it voice and nature will do the rest." That sounds simple enough, does it not? But unfortunately in all the cases I can readily call to mind, nature has had the last word and after being ill-treated for a few short years it has presented its bill for payment, and there being little vocal cash left, the practitioners of the "let nature do its own work" school have been compelled to retire—vocally bankrupt.

There is a technique in singing and it must be acquired. One master of singing has said that technical proficiency in singing may be likened to technique in the playing of other instruments, but there is a difference, for the voice is a living instrument and subject to all the ills and organic changes to which human flesh is heir. Different from all other musical instruments, which are built on definite patterns and in definite shapes, the human voice is a part of one's anatomy and no two human beings are exactly alike, and no one human being is exactly the same throughout his or her life.

It is also true to say that every human voice has an individual quality entirely its own. Through the gift of mimicry we can reproduce the sound and the character of another person's voice but it is never an exact facsimile. Again, the resilience and elasticity of the vocal apparatus or machinery varies enormously, and these variations are mainly physical. Singers who are born with a ready-made perfect vocal machine are very, very rare. Most of us have to overcome some type of psychological or physical defect, and it is to help us to do so that technical exercises have been invented and the practise of them recommended. Technical facility is absolutely essential in order to meet the demands of the music every singer is called upon and required to perform. All the functions of singing have their special techniques, a point I made in the first sentence of this chapter, but since this book is a plain man's guide to singing I do not think I shall be accused of flippancy if I say that the "plain man" usually thinks of technique as the practise of scales and exercises. There are books of vocal exercises ready to hand for the student, compiled by Nava, Concone, Lamperti, Garcia and others, and in addition there are sets of exercises that students are required to learn for the examinations at our schools of music and other examining boards. In my opinion they are often of considerable and unnecessary difficulty, and even when sung with musical accuracy they afford no proof that the student will be equally successful in singing the *fioritura* to be found in the operatic and classical repertoires. Unless studied under the guidance of a thoroughly competent teacher they often do more harm than good. Ffrangcon-Davies in *The Singing of the Future* said, "Scales, like razors, are useful to those who can handle them; but in inexperienced hands they are dangerous." The late Sir Henry J. Wood in his treatise on singing provided a series of exercises that consisted of examples of florid music taken from the works of eminent and established composers—real music that the embryo professional singer would, at some time in his or her career, be asked to perform before an audience. That is the final test, and all exercises should be learned and practised with that goal in view.

One of the fallacies about the teaching of florid vocal technique, and it is a widely prevalent one, is that speed can be attained by, at first, practising slowly. While this is true for instrumental practice it is absolutely and provably wrong in singing. Accuracy, precise intonation and speed can only be attained by practising at a fast tempo, and by the rhythmic and light accentuation of the structural beats of the particular musical passage. One simply cannot learn to sprint by running slowly as a sort of encouragement; it encourages nothing more than heaviness and stiffness of muscular action.

The use of florid exercises can and frequently do extend the range of a voice. The following arpeggio—familiar to students everywhere:

Ah _____

sung *rapidly* on a sweeping out-flow of breath can often enable singers to touch high notes they have never previously attempted.

The speed of the exercise and the springiness of the accent on the first note are the important factors. On no account must there be any attempt to sustain or hold the highest note. Think of the exercise as a musical arch. Drop the jaw a little to make room for the high note, take a full breath, pull in the abdominal muscles, tip the head slightly forward—*not* backward—and let there be no bodily resistance. The speed and the sweep of the outgoing breath will do the rest. This simple arpeggio must of course be sung in keys to suit the voices with which we are dealing. The use of this particular arpeggio exercise is to help one to limber up, as an athlete might say.

I must emphasize that speed is not achieved by physical compulsion; it comes from a mental demand for speed. In simple language, if you desire to sing fast—well—sing fast. If first attempts result in a somewhat smudgy execution of the exercise, do not worry; alternate the vocal sweep with a staccato rendering of the same exercise at a convenient speed; but remember that it must be a *light* staccato.

A helpful exercise is the following:

coo coo coo coo coo coo coo coo coo

every note tapped out on the vowel (the word) "coo", and sung in ascending keys to suit individual voices. This exercise develops a light and free adjustment and approximation of the vocal cords.

No sustained tone exercises should be attempted until at least a degree of vocal flexibility and elasticity has been attained. Slow, sustained exercises if attempted too soon are inclined to place a strain upon the larynx and often lead to muscular stiffness; in other words, the voice itself tends to become bogged down with its own weight and the whole vocal mechanism becomes sluggish.

Another useful exercise sung at a moderate tempo is:

Moderato

ah _____
ee _____
O _____

This exercise should be sung with the accentuation as marked. There should be no special accentuation on the highest note but it should be the climax of the crescendo, and that crescendo should be achieved *entirely* by the out-pouring of the breath. No muscular pressure whatever should be applied. When ascending the scale passage on the vowel "ee" there must on no account be any stiffening of the jaw; in fact a slight *drooping* of the jaw must take place when approaching the highest note, but the will to sing "ee" must remain. The vowel "o" is sung with a rounded mouth and a forward position of the lips.

All vowel sounds are pre-ordained in the mind, and no relaxation of the will to sing a pure vowel sound must be allowed. The mind is, and must ever be, the parent of all the sounds we make.

It is comparatively easy to control the breath when *ascending* a scale because there is a natural increase of vocal tensity; but when descending a scale a tendency to relax the whole vocal apparatus may cause an uncontrolled escapement of breath. To check this fault it is helpful to lift up the chest as the voice descends.

There are many other exercises and there are no fixed rules as to how they should be used or applied because at all times the procedure of tutelage must be adapted to suit individual requirements, and as I have already observed, no two singers are alike. At no stage in the development of a singer should florid exercises be neglected, but I would like to offer this warning: nearly all the published books of vocalise consist of exercises on one selected vowel. I think this is wrong. Exercises on one vowel are by no means easy to sing freely, and the aim of all exercises should be to acquire freedom. It is much better to sing vocal exercises on a series of vowels as a preparation for tackling songs and arias. This advice was given by Fugère, the doyen of the Paris Opera Comique of a past era. I heard this great artist sing at the Opera Comique when he was eighty years of age. Like me, he believed that speech and song were for all practical purposes synonymous terms. So my advice is, begin to use *words* in singing as soon as possible. There are literally dozens of arias by Handel to suit all voices, but do remember, when singing the florid passages, to take the weight off the voice after observing the rhythmic accents:

re - joi - - - - ce

in other words, let the grouped notes spin. Handel wrote supremely well for the human voice and that is why I suggest that in the early stages of training it might be advisable to defer a study of Bach's music until the student's technique has become more assured. Much of Bach's writing for the human voice is very instrumental in character and shape—often of an obbligato character. However, that is by the way and merely a passing comment.

Before I leave the subject of technique I would like to say that weak tones or weak patches in the human voice are not strengthened by continually working on them, and particularly with exercises on sustained tones; indeed, such treatment only makes matters worse, paralysing both the singer's voice and nerve. Short *florid* exercises including the weak notes should restore both confidence and strength:

Bree ___ Brey ___ Brah ___

It is important to remember that the "ey" vowel should have an elbow-touching relationship to the vowel "ee" (see Chapter I).

Now for a few words about the "trill". It has been said by some writers that the practice of the trill is invaluable for all female voices. I maintain that it is invaluable for *all* voices, male and female, and *essential* for all female voices. The trill is a musical ornament that composers use as an added decoration. They would never have added trills to their music if there had not been singers who could execute them. Today, singers who can sing a genuine trill are a rarity. Over and over again I have heard sopranos (professional singers) who in attempting to execute a trill have produced nothing more than a quivering tremolo with a final "turn" to persuade us, or in the hope of persuading us, that the quivering tremolo was a trill. But we are not deceived. A genuine trill is a shaking or oscillation of the voice-box, hence the word "shake" as an alternative one to "trill". In order to acquire a trill, the larynx must be completely free and flexible. A soprano without a trill is one whose technical equipment is suspect—yes, even a dramatic soprano. I well remember Frieda Leider—a great singer who sang the dramatic role of Brünnhilde and the coloratura role of Leonora (*Il Trovatore*) in one season at Covent Garden. An exception? Maybe. But exceptions prove the rule, and the rule is that to be "the compleat singer" one must at least endeavour to acquire a perfect technique.

The successful development of technique is an individual achievement and it is the teacher who can best decide on the most beneficial treatment for each individual case. The teacher will also know that when the pupil has acquired a voice production that is free and physically untrammelled, that pupil will be the better enabled to implement his or her own artistic desires and intentions.

Teaching carries with it grave responsibilities; indeed, it can be said that a teacher (and I am one) who allows a vocal defect to persist can be censured as much as if he had actually taught it.

V

STYLE

"THE STYLE is the man." This is an obvious truth, nor can it be anything else, for as a man is, so must the manner of his expression be. But as there are all sorts of men, so there are all sorts of styles. The cultured man has a cultured style and his personality strikes a note of culture. There are stages in the growth of character and there are also styles that are mature and others that are immature.

The study of style has far too often been turned into a mystery that has about it all the hocus-pocus that we apply to the solving of riddles. Let me try to state a case in simple terms.

Style is a manner of writing, speaking, singing or doing, especially as opposed to the matter to be expressed or to the thing done, hence the phrase, "the style is better than the matter".

We also speak of a florid style, a lucid style or a delightful style. It can be the general characteristics of writing, singing, speaking or of artistic expression; or again, of a way of presenting things proper to a person or school or period or in a manner that rightly exhibits their characteristics. We talk sometimes about "acquiring" a style. Can we? We can cultivate a mannerism or develop an affectation, or by sheer mimicry copy the style we admire in someone else, but we cannot by so doing develop a definite individual personality. Whatever top-surface polish we try to superimpose on ourselves we remain our same basic selves, and so does our style.

Again I say, the style is the man. In Chapter I, I referred to what I regard as the essential bases of good singing, mentioning four in particular; and I have devoted chapters to discussions of them. I also wrote, "There is one other condition, not absolutely essential, but most desirable, and that is personal magnetism. This, however, is a pure gift and I fear can never be acquired." I now add, to become a *great* singer it is not absolutely necessary, because great singers always possess it—it is born in them. Personal magnetism, personality, style, they are all one. We all possess personality in a greater or lesser degree and it is the singer's job to develop his own personality. Read with care these wonderful lines by Walt Whitman:

To a Pupil

Is reform needed? is it through you?

The greater the reform needed, the greater the
Personality you need to accomplish it.

You! do you not see how it would serve to have eyes,
blood, complexion, clean and sweet?

Do you not see how it would serve to have such a body
and soul that when you enter the crowd an atmosphere of desire and command enters with you, and
every one is impress'd with your Personality?

O the magnet! the flesh over and over!

Go, dear friend, if need be give up all else, and commence
today to inure yourself to pluck, reality, self-esteem,
definiteness, elevatedness,

Rest not till you rivet and publish yourself of your own
Personality.

The eloquent force of the last two lines needs no comment.

The word "style" has a variety of meanings, but as I am considering it at this juncture I can define it as the manner of doing a thing and the apparent relish with which it is done. Is it the number of runs made by England's cricket captain, Ted Dexter, that gives his admirers so much joy, or the dashing style with which he makes them? If his cavalier style is not the well-spring of our enjoyment then all the hit-or-miss sloggers who delight the hearts of small boys must be great batsmen.

The courageous and independent singer allows his style to grow with him. As in literature, so in singing, style consists of saying the right thing in the right way and also in the right place. Those singers who confine themselves to one school of music only will never consolidate a convincing style. I have in mind an exclusive group, peculiar to Great Britain, known as Bach singers. As a lover of singing I have always been more interested in the high quality of a performance rather than in the dull performance of high quality music. It is a significant fact, and a sad one, that when candidates turn up at auditions with a list of items consisting of a Bach aria and, say, four art songs, the odds are *at least* fifty to one that the performance will be wretched. The answer is simple. It is a vain attempt by the auditionees to pass themselves off as musical intellectuals. Musical intelligence and taste in the compilation of a programme are admirable things in themselves but what is required of a singer is evidence of the possession of a voice of good quality and some degree of skill in its use. The first lesson all embryo artists should learn is humility. Be true to yourselves and if you can succeed in doing simple things supremely well the day will not be far distant when you can "publish yourself of your own personality" in the greatest works of art.

The singer with style is able to apply the correct treatment to most types of music he is called upon to perform. If, however, for aesthetic reasons he is strongly antipathetic to some particular music or composer he will definitely lose all sense of style whilst attempting to sing a song or a work in which he has no mental or emotional interest. A sense of humility or a realization of one's own technical,

D

musical, emotional or aesthetic limitations is the best way to preserve one's own sense of style.

Music and its performance being more of a mystery to the general
public than talking and acting, it is always possible for a singer to
give a sentimental rendition of classical music and do so persuasively,
particularly if he has a frank, open countenance and an ingratiating
manner. On the other hand, the same public would never tolerate
an actor who applied the same treatment to Shakespeare as he would
to plays by, for instance, John Osborne, Harold Pinter, Arnold
Wesker or Samuel Beckett. All music, whatever its character,
requires understanding and complete sincerity in performance. I
shall have more to say on this subject when we come to discuss
oratorio and opera.

Ffrangcon-Davies said, "the burden laid upon the vocalists of the
future is so to carry out the directions of *bel canto* that nothing written
by the composer shall be considered impossible by the singer." In
the main, this is probably true, but it must be remembered that
Ffrangcon-Davies's active career as a singer was before the days of
serial music and the tone-row composers or before these composers
had the attention of the critics and the *avant garde* of music-lovers.
Like George Bernard Shaw, Ffrangcon-Davies's views of the future
of music did not, quite understandably, extend much further than
Wagner. Had he envisaged some of the vocal contortions and
somersaults which the experimental composers ask singers to perform he might not have said, "whatever a musician can write a
singer can—nay, he must—sing." I cannot believe that he would
have been willing or content to accept whoops and yells as genuine
singing.

Today many composers write with little knowledge of voices,
and such knowledge as they do possess does not extend much beyond
what they imagine to be the characteristics of male and female
voices. They usually know all about the orchestral instruments for
which they write; indeed, no composer of orchestral music would
dream of starting to write without such knowledge. Even when the
music is devoid of original ideas the orchestration is more often than

not teeming with kaleidoscopic instrumental colour. What our modern composers fail to understand is that the human voice has physical limitations. Sopranos, for instance, cannot sing with comfort and ease if they are kept *constantly* ranging round about C to high G with a top A thrown in occasionally. After a while the voice tends to stiffen and the throat tires. The next thing that happens is that they begin to sing out of tune. This has nothing to do with faulty hearing; it is the result of fatigue. A vocal line that has a wide range is far less fatiguing, even though it may look vocally difficult. To put the matter bluntly, the human voice is not an orchestral instrument, and when composers ask singers to make the vowel sounds "ee" and "oo" on extreme high notes they are making unreasonable demands and their music can rightly be called unsingable or unnecessarily difficult. Contemporary singers have some exacting tasks to face, tasks that can be said to "cramp their style", if I may be permitted a colloquial phrase. However, it is up to the professional singer to fit himself to meet the vocal demands of his own day and age. To meet these demands, more than ever must we perfect our technique, and in order to preserve our sense of style we must endeavour to do the right thing in the right way. Fortunately, singers can continue to employ both these attributes in singing a large repertoire of music that is still loved by audiences everywhere. The music of Mozart, Rossini, Verdi, Puccini, Strauss, to mention only a handful of composers, shows no immediate sign of losing its popularity. All this music calls for real singing, polished technique and, I must say it again, a sense of style.

"The style is the man", and in the music of the future, man has some problems to solve.

VI

ORATORIO

Most of us think we know what we mean when we use the word "oratorio" but in fact it is a term difficult to define. In different countries and at different periods it has had many meanings. Today we think of an oratorio as a musical setting of a religious story or narrative for chorus, orchestra, and solo singers and intended for performance in concert halls or churches. But it was not always so; indeed, we know that many of Handel's so-called oratorios were planned and written for stage performances. On the other hand, Haydn's *The Seasons* is an oratorio (he called it so) but piety is not a marked feature of the libretto. Oratorio, like opera, began in Italy but it owes its genesis to Sacred Mysteries and Miracle Plays popular long years ago all over Europe. Also we must not forget the part St. Philip Neri (1515–95) played in the popularizing of musical services in buildings other than churches. Romance has described the venue of his spiritual and musical ministrations as taking place "in a top back room" but in fact they were held in an oratory, and these early musical evenings led to the founding of a religious order, the "Congregation of the Oratory", known today as The Oratorians. Cardinal Newman was an Oratorian and it was his deeply moving poem *The Dream of Gerontius* that inspired Sir Edward Elgar to compose one of the greatest oratorios of the twentieth century.

Some of the most illustrious composers in the world have contributed magnificently to the rich library of music that rightly and properly comes under the category of oratorios. Here is a sheaf of outstanding names: Schutz, J. S. Bach, C. P. E. Bach, Handel, Haydn, Beethoven, Spohr, Liszt, Graun, Dvořák, Berlioz, Franck, Pierné, Honegger, Martin, Elgar, Howells and Tippett.

I must confess to some feelings of trepidation in presenting my thoughts and views about oratorio to a present-day audience of readers, because we are living in a pagan age, when Christian ethics and traditions which are the basis of our civilization are not only being fiercely disputed but often openly rejected. It is indeed a critical hour in the story of our race and unless we can recover the faith of our fathers it is quite conceivable that the moral structure of society will collapse in ruins. Whether one regards this possibility as a misfortune or a promise of better things to come is a matter for one's own individual thinking. I regard the crisis as part of the combative glory to live. History is cyclic and what is out-of-date thinking today is the new thought of tomorrow. However, it is significant to note that there are fewer oratorios performed today than there were twenty years ago and maybe fewer actual performances of oratorios as a type of musical work. Let me explain this somewhat cryptic remark. There are hundreds of annual performances of Handel's *Messiah*, but what of his other oratorios?—very few. Haydn's *Creation* is still quite popular, but *Elijah* (Mendelssohn), once a great favourite, is heard less and less. On the other hand, Bach's *St. Matthew Passion* is challenging *Messiah* for the position of top of the poll. Bach's *St. John Passion* is performed only occasionally, and as for Handel's *Passion*, I had a hand, when an official with the B.B.C., in its revival after years of neglect.

Elgar's *The Dream of Gerontius* continues to grip the imagination and the affection of the British public, but his two more conventional

oratorios, namely *The Apostles* and *The Kingdom*, are seldom performed. The religious work that excites the public more than any
other is Verdi's *Requiem*, but this work is essentially operatic in
style.

To sum up the position, we may get a goodly number of performances of oratorio each year but the repertoire of works performed
has shrunk.

There is a school of musical criticism that is hostile to oratorio
as an art form. Aaron Copland, the doyen of American composers
and a very distinguished one, when writing (in his book *Copland on
Music*) about Hindemith's first essay in the field of oratorio, *Das
Unaufhörliche*, expressed astonishment that the mood Hindemith
created "was not very different from what Brahms or Mahler
might have given us with the same text." To have done even that
would, in my opinion, have been a considerable achievement, but
Aaron Copland has very different views, and he goes on to say:
"We were presented with a work that was in every respect an
oratorio, the dear old dead oratorio with its sanctimonious and
familiar stench." "Stench"! That is an unpleasant word, but if
anyone believes that oratorio is dead and is in a state of decomposi-
tion it is, for them, the right word. I am reminded of Longfellow's
The Golden Legend and the words he put into the mouth of Lucifer,
"There is in the air . . . an odour of innocence and of prayer . . . I
cannot breathe such an atmosphere." If a singer cannot breathe such
an atmosphere let him spare himself the discomfort of singing
oratorio and spare us the discomfort of having to listen to him.

Peter Heyworth, the music critic of the *Observer*, a Sunday paper
notable for its Liberal political views and its rationalism, had this to
say about a concert of twentieth-century music to celebrate the
B.B.C's fortieth birthday: "The atavistic eruptions that shook the
Festival Hall last Wednesday . . . provided a disturbing glimpse
into the bowels of our turbulent age." It is highly probable that a
large percentage of the audience could not breathe freely in this
Freudian atmosphere. I am innocent enough to believe that Bach's
B minor Mass is of more spiritual worth to troubled minds than

anything to be found in the Nietzsche-inspired *Mass of Life* by Delius. The hope of the world is that God—not man—has the last word.

Oratorio as we know it and accept it, is, as I have already said, the musical setting of biblical narratives and stories about the sublimity and the power of the Christian faith. Such passion as is engendered is of the spiritual type with more psychic than physical qualities. It has been said by more than one writer that the loftier the theme, the purer the music; but alas, this has not always been the case. In Victorian times, in Great Britain at any rate, there were many oratorios composed that were not only extremely dull but musically meretricious. Nevertheless, if composers cannot always rise to the sublimity of a chosen theme, it is incumbent on the singer at least to make an attempt to do so. He must at all times endeavour to rise above himself. The message, the meaning and the colour of words must be his first and only consideration. The strictly objective approach is the only permissible one. "Thus saith the Lord, the Lord of Hosts." Not I, not you or the other fellow, but "The Lord". What did He say? "Yet once, a little while, and I will shake the heav'ns, and the earth, the sea, and the dry land." If we sing these words with conviction and with the timbre which suits the character of the words we can capture the attention of the audience immediately—the effect will be electric. Another familiar recitative from *Messiah* is "For behold, darkness shall cover the earth". The correct and appropriate timbre of voice is vitally important here, but in trying to convey and will an atmosphere of foreboding do not "mouth" and cover the tone to such an extent that the words come out something like this: "Fur be-hurld dorkness shall cor-vor the orth." If you do—and how often have we heard it done so—the desired effect and meaning of the words will be lost entirely.

The elements of good oratorio singing are these: a strict regard for the composer's music and an intense belief in the divine truth of the message or story to be conveyed to the audience. In the older oratorios a few words "oft repeated" served as the lyric for a solo, but in spite of this literary non-inventiveness and the monotony of the repetitions, it is possible to make this mannered music sound as if it were the only possible way to set the words; indeed, it should be made to sound inevitable. The stricter and more rigid the musical form the more intense must be the understanding behind the words, otherwise there is always a chance that the body of the message will be lost in the folds of the musical costume.

The singing of the arias, speaking generally, is governed by the laws of *bel canto* and the sincerity of one's mental approach. Practically all the arias in oratorio are pictorial comments on the narrative and as such should be treated as songs to be sung beautifully and in a human way. One may find this a matter of difficulty in certain circumstances. We suffer a good deal in this day and age from the tyranny of purists of the pedantic sort, whose pettifogging strictures are having the effect of taking the life-blood out of the art of free and untrammelled singing. It is salutary to remind ourselves that most of the oratorios we hear frequently today were written at a time in musical history when the composers were content, with all reasonable safeguards, to allow the solo singers a free hand. What they asked of them was to sing the music with all the beauty, charm and vocal artifice at their command. In this way the music—the arias, I mean—lived their own life, free and unfettered; they arose, as it were, out of the dramatic situation. These situations are an inherent part of the story or narrative and are declaimed musically in recitative which is, of course, the dialogue which keeps the story in motion. Pages and pages have been written by various professors about the singing of recitative and I have even been told by my professional confrères that So-and-So is marvellous at teaching recitative. A singer who has to be taught how to sing recitative has no sense of acting and he should never be entrusted with the job of telling a story in song.

"Oh", I can hear some contentious person saying, "why do you use the phrase 'sense of acting' when writing about the singing of oratorio? Oratorio and opera are completely different fields of expository activity." Are they different? I do not think so, where truth of declamation is concerned. But it may be said, the style is different. Now what is meant by this off-hand remark? Is it postulated that the religious character of oratorio calls for a super-imposed ecclesiastical manner and demeanour? If so, I cannot accept this point of view. Nothing has done more to depopularize oratorio in Great Britain than the smugness of the solo-performers. We have grown weary of the seraphic sopranos and lachrymose contraltos gazing out into the concert hall as if in a trance or as if looking for the lost horizon. These airs of false sanctimony are not only devitalizing, they are positively boring. Truth and style are one, and true declamation, be the subject-matter sacred or profane, carries its own style.

The singing of recitative should be "governed primarily by common sense". This was the opinion of the late Harry Plunket-Greene, and there was very little about interpretation that he did not know.

The inability to sing recitative seems confined to British singers, although we have, of course, many fine artists in this country to whom this remark does not apply. I have never heard even third-rate singers in France and Germany who could not tackle a recitative intelligently. The answer to this is that other nations take a pride in speaking their mother tongue and we do not.

There are two kinds of recitative, the "free" and the "accompanied". The accompanied recitative is indistinguishable from an air, except that the singer will perhaps line in a phrase or word here and there to mark a point in the narrative. The recitative proper requires freedom of delivery—by that I do not mean the singer should be permitted to run amuck. No! the music must keep its shape and its rhythm as far as the bars are concerned, but within the bar freedom is allowed, in order to declaim with true dramatic sense. When a composer writes a recitative he does little more than *indicate* what he requires of the singer. He does not expect his notes to be altered but his note-values may be, to fit the various individual ideas of how the speech should be declaimed. It will be admitted that no two actors would speak the narrative or plot-lines in Shakespeare's plays in *exactly* the same way, and the same thing applies to a recitative in singing. I have said, "A singer who has to be taught how to sing recitative has no sense of acting." Well, I suppose we cannot all be actors, so let me give an example of what must not be done in recitative singing. I will take the recitative that precedes the baritone solo, "The Trumpet Shall Sound" from Handel's *Messiah*:

Recitative.—BEHOLD, I TELL YOU A MYSTERY.

This is what it *usually* sounds like (the words in block type represent long notes): "Behold, I TELL you a MYS-te-REE, we shall not ALL sleep, but WE shall all be CHANG'D (comma) in a mo-MENT, in the twinkling OF an eye AT the last trum-PET."

Nothing could be more wrong. The natural and, I think, the truest way to sing and phrase the recitative is as follows:

The words, "but we shall all be chang'd in a moment" must be sung in one continuous phrase. In the last word, "trumpet", the "R" must be rolled. A slight slowing-up is permissible in the last bar, to give emphasis to the words.

Take particular note that the recitative is an accompanied one, and nothing whatever in my rephrasing interferes with the rhythm and time-values of the accompaniment.

Considering still further some of the problems of recitative, it is sometimes essential not only to rephrase but actually to alter the notes in order to get the English accents in the right place. There are numerous instances of this "editing" in Bach's *St. Matthew Passion* in rendering the original German into English.

One of the oratorios I particulary have in mind is Haydn's *Creation*. Here are two specimen instances of recitatives crying out for alteration:

As printed in the Vocal Score:

RAPHAEL

And God made the fir-ma-ment, and di-vi-ded the wa-ters which were under the firmament from the waters which were a-bove the fir-ma-ment: and it was so.

Suggested re-phrasing:

As printed in the Vocal Score:

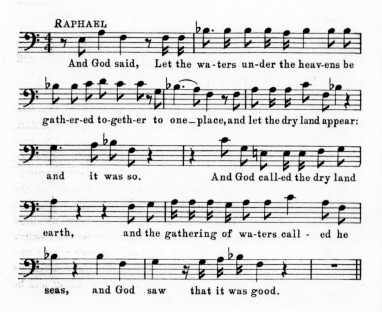

Suggested re-phrasing:

Years ago oratorio singers and opera singers were, for all practical purposes, almost entirely different types of people and they seldom encroached upon each other's professional territory—Sims Reeves and Sir Charles Santley being outstanding exceptions. I have an ineffaceable memory of hearing Santley sing "Why do the nations" in the Philharmonic Hall, Liverpool. He was an old man, but the vigour, the fire and the technical precision of his singing was something that, in my judgment, has never been equalled by any other bass or baritone of whom I have any knowledge. However, Santley was, like all great singers, a law unto himself. He didn't have one manner for oratorio and another for opera. He was eminent in both fields of musical activity because he was a fine singer and he had the courage of his artistic opinions.

Nowadays there is a greater measure of free-trade amongst singers, and although the typical oratorio ones are not, as a rule, very effective on the operatic stage, the opera singers have brought an invigorating breeze into the atmosphere of oratorio. A wit made the remark that the English loved performances of oratorio because they gave them all the spiritual uplift of a church service without the inconvenience of a collection. Since there has been a falling-off in church attendance there has also been a falling-off in the demand for oratorio; but happily the best and the most vital of the spiritual and cultural organizations of our society survive and are the better and the stronger for the fight to do so.

The decline in the demand for oratorio has coincided with the ever-increasing demand for opera.

VII

OPERA

It is not my purpose to write a précis of the history of opera, nor is this the book in which to make the attempt. It is sufficient for us to know that the earliest opera of which we have the complete music is Peri's *Euridice*, some portions of which were supplied by Caccini; the date is 1600 and the place Venice. Three hundred and sixty-three years is not a long span of history, and when we remember that the "new art of opera" did not reach England until 1656 the historical perspective is further reduced.

The creative contributions of the English-speaking world to opera, when compared to those of Italy, Germany and Austria and France are, I am afraid, very meagre. It would not be too sweeping a statement to say that after Purcell and then Handel there has not been anyone of comparable stature to Rossini, Bellini, Meyerbeer, Weber, Wagner, Verdi, Puccini, Bizet, Massenet, Humperdinck or Richard Strauss until the arrival of Benjamin Britten. It is true that we have had a number of distinguished British composers who have written operas—Balfe, Wallace, Benedict, Goring Thomas, Stanford, Sullivan, Smyth, Delius, Boughton, Vaughan Williams and

51

others—but none of their operas have found a fixed place in the repertoire of opera companies either in Great Britain or anywhere else. Arthur Sullivan is the one exception, but his operettes are in a category of their own and it is true to say that, collectively, they are a cul-de-sac in operatic history. It has been estimated that upwards of forty-four thousand operas and operettes have been written and that through the years the number of people who have spent the major part of their lives singing and dabbling in opera approximates to the total population of a sizeable town. Like moths around a flame, singers the world over cannot resist the dazzle of opera, and even though they burn their vocal wings they must keep on fluttering round and round.

When I was a scholar at the Royal College of Music many years ago it seemed to me that all my fellow singing students had one aim and object in life, and that was to sing in opera. It was a strange ambition in view of the fact that there were so few opportunities at that time for any singers to exhibit their powers in opera.

Let us glance at the state of operatic affairs in Great Britain fifty years ago. There were the annual international seasons at Covent Garden in the spring, when a British singer could consider him or herself very lucky if he or she managed to secure an engagement to play even a small part. In the big provincial towns and the suburbs of London there were visits to the local theatres by the Carl Rosa Opera Company and the Moody-Manners Opera Company and, forty years ago, the British National Opera Company. The smaller provincial towns depended for their opera on the J. W. Turner Opera Company, the Nielson, the Gilbert and the Rowsby companies, and later we had the O'Mara Company.

The performances by the Carl Rosa, the Moody-Manners and the British National opera companies were on the whole pretty good, and amongst the principals there were some very distinguished artists. The small opera companies put on performances that were rough-and-ready hit-or-miss affairs, with hotch-potch orchestras, but whatever they lacked in finesse and external adornments they were certainly not lacking in vocal power and uninhibited enthusiasm. It was the age when the audiences expected to hear big, strong voices in opera.

Those who had not big enough voices devoted themselves to oratorio and ballad concerts and usually secured for themselves a longer and more lucrative career than the overworked and underpaid touring opera singers.

That a voluminous voice was considered to be the primary essential in anyone aspiring to become a successful opera singer was amply confirmed by a celebrated music-hall comedian of the last generation, namely, Wilkie Bard. That famous droll delighted audiences with a song in which he, in a hoarse and confidential voice, imparted to us the secret of his life, which was, "I want to sing in opera". The absurdity of the situation was not lost upon even the dullest of his hearers.

In his quaint way Mr. Wilkie Bard was unwittingly singing the swan song of the tyrannical supremacy of the singer in the operatic world. Today we do not think of opera as a vehicle specially designed for the exhibition of loud-voiced singers, supported by a non-partisan, static chorus, and set against a pictorial background of a city or pastoral glade of a neutral and hitherto unknown country. Singers are no longer in sole charge of the proceedings. Gluck was the first composer to strike a blow in the cause of dramatic truth, or what should more accurately be described as the *restoration* of dramatic truth in opera. It was a long fight, but it eventually led to Wagner's conception of music-drama and to our conception of opera as an art-form, a combination of several forms of art; vocal, orchestral, dramatic writing, *mise-en-scène* of the theatre, stage production and finally, the over-all claims of the composer's music. If the music of an opera fails, everything else fails; indeed, there is no case on record where a poor score has been saved by the cleverness of the libretto, a slick stage production, imaginative scenery, astonishing singing or brilliant conducting. An opera stands or falls by the intrinsic quality and dramatic truth of its music. Great works of art in music can stand almost any treatment and survive.

E

The greatest operas, those that have stood the test of time and the changes of fashion, have all been written by men who not only had something worthwhile to say for themselves as composers *per se*, but who knew how to write for the theatre, which is, in the operatic sense, an academy of the arts. Apropos this statement, and as I have already made a passing reference to Benjamin Britten earlier in this chapter, I think it should be noted, with a sense of national pride, that *his* operas have found immediate acceptance in opera houses in many countries. But this is not very surprising, because although they are written in a contemporary musical idiom they are singable, practical and tremendously effective in the theatre, the enviroment for which they were planned and written. In short, they are real operas and they have made their indelible impact because they are written by a man who understands the theatre and knows how to write music for singers to sing. Let me repeat—*music for singers to sing*; that is the point I wish to stress and since this book is about singing, it is this aspect of opera that is our chief concern.

Aaron Copland said of Britten's operas that they "show every sign of being carefully planned from first word to final note. Nothing is left to chance . . . Probably the most striking single factor in his operatic writing is the richness, variety, breadth and sweep of his melodic lines."

"Music for singers to sing" and "breadth of melodic lines"— these two phrases contain in themselves the secret of how to write effectively for the theatre with any hope of lasting success. If, on the other hand, we envisage a time when opera will have thrown overboard the idea of singing as a means of emotional and dramatic expression, regarding it as an outmoded medium, we need not bother any further about how to apply the art of singing to the demands of opera. We have had, during the past few years, some examples of experimental writing for the human voice in the field of opera, but judging by the special pleading and the careful statements of the critics, who must guard themselves against *possible* error, and on the other side, the ill-disguised hostility of the audience, I cannot believe the so-called melodic lines resembling the temperature chart of a patient in a feverish condition have come to stay.

There is still a market for Gluck, Rameau, Bellini, Donizetti, Rossini, Mozart, Beethoven, Wagner, Verdi, Bizet, Debussy, Moussorgsky, Puccini, Massenet, Richard Strauss, Ravel, Janaček, Stravinsky and Bartók. (The latter composer's one-act opera *Bluebeard's Castle* is one of considerable vocal beauty.) With such a rich store of operas available to the steadily-increasing number of people who want to hear them for the aesthetic reward or the mere emotional enjoyment they get by frequenting the opera houses, the prospects for the singers who "want to sing in opera" have increased four-fold.

For the first time in our history we in Britain now have a national opera; in using that term I mean an organization or organizations subsidized from public funds. The two organizations or establishments are The Royal Opera House, Covent Garden and the Sadler's Wells Opera Company. These two companies are each controlled by separate boards of directors and both companies draw financial aid from H.M. Treasury through the auspices of The Arts Council of Great Britain, which in many respects functions as a Ministry of Fine Arts.

There are, of course, the Royal Ballet and the School of Ballet and several other cultural activities relating to the theatre but they are outside the range of this particular book and I merely mention them in passing.

Here we are then: We have at last two full-sized opera companies in London operating throughout the year and together employing a large number of singers. In addition there is opera at Glyndebourne for a limited season each year, and these annual operatic festivals have found favour with connoisseurs all over the world. Although the Glyndebourne seasons are planned on international lines many British singers are given opportunities to play principal roles and some have done so with outstanding success.

In short, the ever-increasing public interest in opera following, as it did, the amazing nation-wide interest in ballet since the last world war, has completely revolutionized the whole pattern of our musical life. The Sadler's Wells Company does not only supply opera in English for London but it has also a company touring the provinces, the principal singers of both companies being interchangeable. The Royal Opera House Company does not confine itself to opera in English; the performances are given in the language that the management considers most suitable to the particular opera and the particular cast engaged to perform the work. The carrying-out of this policy, and I consider it a wise one, means that the resident English-speaking artists are required to sing in, maybe, three and sometimes four languages. If these conditions seem unduly exacting for British opera singers compared to those of their confrères in Italy, France and Germany, it must not be forgotten that in the three countries I have named opera *has* a tradition and *is* a tradition; and furthermore, all three countries have big enough repertoires of national major operatic works to enable them to keep their opera houses open without the urgent need of importations. However, the sheer necessity of having to learn operatic roles in languages other than their own has been, to what is in fact a new race of English-speaking opera singers, a blessing in disguise, even if a hard-won blessing.

The days of the one-way traffic of European opera singers to English-speaking countries is over; the traffic continues to flow but it is no longer one-way. To use a current phrase, a common market is in operation. Many singers from Great Britain, Canada, Australasia and the U.S.A. have found employment in European opera houses, not only as guest artists for special roles but as singers holding staff contracts.

I think it is true to say that the American singers have led the way in this free trade movement. There were (1962) no fewer than 120 Americans on the rolls of the opera houses of Germany and Austria.

One of the most significant features of the opera house policy of the Covent Garden and Sadler's Wells managements has been the influx of admirable voices from Australia and Canada, some of whom quickly achieved international reputations, notably Joan Sutherland and Jon Vickers.

Of the home-bred singers one cannot fail to mention Geraint Evans who, starting his career at the Royal Opera House, Covent Garden, is now an artist of international standing and who, in singing at La Scala, followed in the footsteps—after many long years—of the great Sir Charles Santley. Then again there is the outstanding success of Richard Lewis.

The prospects for those who wish to make a career in opera have never been so bright as they are today, but—and now comes the snag—it is no use thinking about such ideas unless one possesses the right size and type of voice for the job. Time and time again during my lifetime young people have told me that they wish to study for an operatic career, but alas, in the majority of cases it is sufficient to hear them sing one operatic aria to know at once that they do not possess either the voice or the temperament to permit them even to dream about attempting to fulfil their ambitions.

We have all heard the phrase "an operatic style" but what does it mean? It is extremely difficult to define with any precision but I would say that it is something akin to the method employed by a painter in oils when he tackles a large canvas. To my mind it is a method or technique that consists of broad sweeps, highlights and sharp contrasts. It is the possession of an instinctive sense of the theatre, the very smell of the place that causes the nerves to tingle the moment one enters through the Stage Door.

Opera houses are large buildings and the most successful performers in them are extroverts with outsize personalities. It is true that there are operas that call for subtle delineations of character but these works are exceptions. The normal operatic repertoire calls for a display of histrionics on a grand scale—one meaning of the term "Grand Opera".

As recently as December 1962 I saw these headlines in two of our national daily papers: "Opera Heroine Eschews Histrionics" and "A Tosca free from Melodrama". Astonishing statements indeed. Tosca without histrionics and free from melodrama! Why? Puccini's opera *Tosca*, a setting of a libretto deriving from Sardou's play *Tosca*, *is* a melodrama and the wishful thinking of critics cannot transmute it into anything else. If ever there was a melodramatic author it was Sardou, and as an opera composer Puccini's supreme mastery of this craft has never been in dispute.

The histrionics of the operatic stage call for a different technique from that of the spoken drama. Sung music, except in recitative, slows up movement and the pace of the speech, and the naturalness often aimed at in the performance of plays is not possible in opera. It is probably because of this that we have suffered so long from that meaningless arm-waving that some opera singers fondly imagine is a dramatic gesture. Happily, the era when singing meant everything and acting less than nothing has almost passed away; but the problem of finding a convincing amalgam of both styles (speech and song) is still with us. It is being solved gradually by producers who are sensitive to the histrionic limitations placed upon them by the music itself, in relation to what might loosely be described as time and space.

It is a difficult problem for producers because although we all agree that opera as an art form is a combination of several arts, the music is, as I have already said, the most important factor; by which I mean the quality of the music and the expertise of its performance. Good orchestral playing we expect and get, and allowing for the inevitable "off days" it is never less than professionally competent. The singing, on the other hand, varies a good deal both in quality of vocal tone and technical accomplishment. It can never be otherwise because we are dealing with human beings performing on a human instrument.

Thirty years ago the drawing power of opera depended largely on the brilliance of its star performers. To some considerable extent this is so today, not only in opera but in the theatre, the cinema and TV; nevertheless, there is an insistent demand for a higher standard of performance from the entire ensemble. This is a very healthy artistic trend and holds in itself an encouragement to all the up-and-coming young opera singers.

Each field of vocal activity has its own standard repertoire but such is the magnetic attraction of opera that this is the one that is best known to singers everywhere. The famous arias from the operas of all nations have been known to every student of singing for a hundred years at least, and therefore we need not stop on the road to discuss all the essential vocal requirements for even an adequate performance of any one of them. The matter can be summed up by saying, a good resonant voice, complete freedom of breathing and production, freedom of articulation and declamation and an inborn sense of how to address oneself to an audience. "Back-room boys" in politics, the law and commerce have their uses, but "back-room boys" in the world of operatic *singing* are "also-rans", or even worse, "non-starters"!

Since the operas in the standard repertoire are familiar fare to us all we should, I think, take a look at what is demanded of singers by modern composers. By modern composers I mean those who have discarded the creative techniques of a long apostolic succession of composers that culminated, roughly speaking, with Richard Strauss. Benjamin Britten is a modern but I think it will be found that his music stems from the old apostolic root and therein lies its strength and the likelihood of its survival.

Here are three examples of the sort of thing singers are asked to tackle:

MOSES AND AARON, Schönberg

wenn Mo-ses von die-ser Hö-he___ her-nie-der-steigt,

Wo ihm al-lein das___ Ge-setz sich of-fen - bart.

LULU, Alban Berg

Oh, ich weiss es wohl was aus mir ge-hor der wa-re__

__ wenn Sie mich nicht da - vor

ELEGY FOR YOUNG LOVERS, Hans Werner Henze

My__ Lord, my yearn - ing, as you will it

and will need me like tod-dy__ on re - turn-ing, I

stay_____ as you knew me

These strange leaps and bounds are sometimes described as *canti-lena*; but whatever we think of them, or how unvocal we find them to be, it is the singer's task to make them sound natural and musically inevitable. Or, to put the matter another way, he or she must try to make the abnormal sound normal.

Opera, like any other creative activity, must come to grips with the age in which it lives and has its being, and the work of the Dode-caphonic and Tone-Row composers is intended to be in tune with the restless and changing world in which we now find ourselves. Be that as it may, some of the operatic works by the *avant garde* presented for our approval have been acclaimed by critics not so much because of their importance as dramatic and musical art but because, as bulldozers, they "break new ground" and therefore are more to be commended than, say, *Der Rosenkavalier* which some of us, myself included, are moronic enough actually to like.

Is the musical language we have known and which we understand a dead one? That is a question for each of us to answer for ourselves. What we do know is that there are sufficient operas in a musical language which the great mass of the public *do* understand to keep the opera singers of the world busy in this generation and the next. Whether a "twelve-note serial" will sustain us on the road to an, as yet, unexplored musical country I do not know, but it may well be that as we, the singers, journey on the road to Parnassus this song will ring in our ears:

A Note About the Singing of Gilbert and Sullivan.

When speaking about Sullivan operettes in the early part of this chapter I said that they are in a category of their own and that collectively they are a cul-de-sac in operatic history. This, of course, is a generally accepted fact but since the copyright on the Gilbert and Sullivan operas has now expired the exclusive rights to professional performances has passed away from the D'Oyly Carte Opera Company and performances are now being given by other organizations, notably by the Sadler's Wells Company.

This company is taking the Gilbert and Sullivan operettes, one by one, into its repertoire with highly satisfactory box-office results. The artistic results may for some time be a matter for dispute, because although the critics have for many years been saying that these little works of theatrical art would be all the better for some "spring-cleaning", which would rid the performances of the cob-webs of so-called tradition, the attempts to carry this out are giving rise to doubts in the minds of the critics and the public alike as to whether the cleaning operations are really necessary and whether they are having the desired effect. The moment the well-intentioned improvers set to work on reproducing the Gilbert and Sullivan operettes they came up against a serious and almost insurmountable difficulty, which to the credit of the producers they frankly admit. That difficulty is simply this: These operettes are gems of theatrical construction. Now, whether you like them or not—to quote W. S. Gilbert—"it really doesn't matter". What *does* matter is that you cannot fiddle about with them without running the risk of destroy-ing them. The Gilbert and Sullivan operettes are perfect works of art of their particular kind, and although I have said in published articles and lectures that they are strong enough to withstand almost any treatment, to be seen and appreciated at their true worth they must be interpreted as Gilbert and Sullivan intended them to be interpreted. Their intentions can be expressed in the words that Shakespeare put into the mouth of Hamlet in his instructions to the Players: "Speak the speech, I pray you, as I pronounced it to you, trippingly on the tongue . . . Nor do not saw the air too much with your hand . . . suit the action to the word, the word to the action . . and let those that play your clowns speak no more than is set down for them".

These lines might have been written by Sir William Gilbert him-self, for it is a matter of stage history that in the theatre he was a martinet, and the actors had to speak his words as he wrote them and in the way he wanted them spoken; furthermore, he demanded a clarity of articulation from his singers never known before his time and not often forthcoming since. The whole secret of the art (or skill, if you prefer that word) of performing Gilbert and Sullivan is the full realization of the fact that the words and the music are a perfect and indissoluble unity: $G+S = S+G$.

The detractors of the D'Oyly Carte traditional style of perform-ance have often thought, and indeed said, that Sullivan's music in the operettes has not been given the respect it deserves. To some extent this may be true, particularly from the orchestral point of view; but to treat the vocal music as some of the Mozartian pedants (pedants, mark you, not lovers) are attempting to do, is wrong. The *bel canto* approach is, for the most part, required from the principal sopranos and tenors, nearly all the other roles are played, or should be played, by singing-actors with gifts for characterization. *All* are required to sing in a truly vocal way (*and* in tune!) both in solos and ensembles, but the actual performance of the roles as individual characters in the play is and must be the first consideration. "Readings" and "interpretations" of the Gilbert and Sullivan roles by star operatic singers are not required; they upset the delicate balance of the constructional pattern of the operettes. What is needed are well-schooled, disciplined singers who can speak and sing the English language in a way that will transmit its meaning, its inflexions and its innuendos with a compelling immediacy. It has been said time and again that the Gilbert and Sullivan operettes are fool-proof and the enthusiastic amateur operatic companies everywhere are witnesses of the fact that if any body of singing-actors are content to speak and sing what Gilbert and Sullivan have set down for them to do, and follow the prompt book or book of instructions, a presentable performance can be achieved. Nevertheless, the better the individual ability and quality of the performers, the better the result.

I have had a lengthy experience of playing roles in Gilbert and Sullivan (mostly the character-comedy roles) for the Gramophone Company (H.M.V.) dating from 1917 to 1962, and the sole explanation for my exceptionally long reign as an active performer has been my ability to sing the patter songs not only with mechanical rapidity (that is not sufficient) but with inflexional sense and meaning; what I describe as a real and true *parlando*, which is the ability or trick, or whatever you like to call it, of *talking* on a tune. Judging by the number of years I have held my own as a specialist, I am forced to believe it is a rare gift! A singer without any understanding of what *parlando* really means is the wrong choice for roles in Gilbert and Sullivan operettes.

Sing and act them for all they are worth; they are worth a great deal. Savour the wit and humour; understand its meaning and make it meaningful; and I might add the salutary warning to the comedians that wit cannot be caricatured. The Gilbert and Sullivan operettes have stood the test of over eighty years' hard wear and tear, and their hold upon the affections of the public, both here and in the U.S.A., is a happy augury for their survival.

VIII

THE VOICE AND THE
MICROPHONE

In these days when so many of the utilitarian functions of our
daily lives are governed and controlled by electronics, no book
about singing would be complete without some reference to the
making of gramophone records and broadcasting, since the special
technique required for the carrying-out of these assignments are for
all practical purposes alike.

My knowledge of mechanical reproductions of the human voice
dates back to 1909; in other words, I have been making gramophone
records covering a period of fifty-four years, and have been a broadcaster since 1924. In the field of gramophone recording my experience harks back to the days of acoustical recording, known as the
"tin trumpet" era, when it was said that unless a voice was a hundred
per cent gramophonic it was no use to the gramophone companies.
The unsuccessful ones used to say that the making of gramophone
records was a trick, and that some of the worst singers were good
recorders. The making of gramophone records was not a trick,
although a certain amount of specialized technique had to be
learned.

That some of the good recorders were not outstandingly success-ful on the concert platform was true enough but all of them had real voices. A good, honest voice was a gramophonic voice. One of the pioneers of the gramophone industry in this country told me years ago that all the singers he had "snapped up" for recording purposes had eventually become famous. Here is a short list of some of the recording singers of the "acoustical" days in Great Britain: John McCormack, John Harrison, Ernest Pike, Peter Dawson, Robert Radford, Harry Dearth, Stanley Kirkby, Hubert Eisdell, Albert Whelan, Sir Henry Lytton, Sir Harry Lauder, Kirkby Lunn, Agnes Nicholls and Edna Thornton. There are, of course, others too, but those I have mentioned were real recording artists, could sing anything (and did) and all achieved some measure of fame. I have not included Melba because her records are not replicas of herself as a great singer. She never troubled to make them so.

The best imitations of Harry Lauder that were ever made on records were made by Peter Dawson under the name of Hector Grant. I myself have sung under so many names that I have difficulty in remembering them all. Those were the days when perfect record-ing voices were in short supply.

Since the introduction of the microphone and electrical recording it is possible to make records of any voice; but the best voices still make the best records, always provided that the possessor of the good voice is able to infuse personality into his singing.

It requires great concentration and will-power to impress one's personality on an unseen audience, for one has no stage-accessories to help one, no magnetism of a visible audience, none of that thrill that is inseparable from public performance.

If a singer's voice falls pleasantly on the ear and his articulation is clear he will attract the attention of his unseen audience at once; how long he will retain its attention depends on the quality or type of the music sung and the conviction with which it is sung. It is true that popular sentimental flapdoodle "gets over" with the class of people who like that kind of thing and have contracted a mania for that sort of song; but the rule stands. There is another and most important art to cultivate if one wishes to command the ears of the unseen audience (or any audience) and that is the art of inflexions. A good voice, clear articulation and sincerity are splendid attributes, but without the artist's subtle sense of inflexions a singer sooner or later becomes a bore.

All the great actors and all the great public speakers of the world possess this priceless quality but I am afraid it is not common to all the so-called great singers, certainly not all the great opera singers. The art, the use and the control of inflexions is of itself the very essence of singing and is invaluable to anyone addressing an audience through the medium of the microphone, whether singing or speaking. The microphone is like a powerful lens on a camera, it shows up all our technical faults remorselessly; that is why there will always be a market for the artist-singer whatever developments in mechanical reproduction the future holds in store. However, radio supremacy is not won by vocal technique alone. There must be the indefinable something extra, or ear-catching mannerism, that proclaims itself as soon as the singing-actor makes himself or herself heard. It is a star-quality possessed by few. I listen to many broadcasts each week, and to few of the singers I hear would I give a "star rating".

The microphone can be, and is, a great help to a singer in that it makes him clean up his technique. Hoarseness, faulty intonation, slovenly attack, throatiness, careless articulation, chopping phrases instead of singing them, tobogganing one's way through a song and untidiness generally; all these things are laid bare by the microphone. Although platform tricks are of no assistance in microphone work, either recording or broadcasting, the performance must not become dull and lifeless on account of the absence of a visible audience. The singer who allows this to happen is a failure as a broadcaster. Facial play that mirrors the workings of the mind will be heard in the voice quite unmistakably by the unseen audience. A lively imagination and intense concentration are absolute essentials.

Whispering singers can be amplified, especially with the use of the "echo chamber", but one's ear can detect the amplified voice, and I do not regard it as genuine singing; it can be effective over the radio but I hold the view that fake singing is not necessary or desirable in the present advanced stage of wireless engineering. Maybe I am prejudiced on this point, because I am not a whispering broadcaster. Except for the observance of the elementary rules of microphone technique, all the really famous radio artists sing in the broadcasting studio exactly as they would in the concert hall.

From the strictly vocal point of view there is a very serious side to the question of adapting one's voice to suit the microphone. Constant singing in half-voice relaxes the whole vocal apparatus to such an extent that the power to sing in the normal and natural way is lost, and the voice will gradually die through lack of use; or more accurately, it will perish through improper use.

The perfect broadcast is the one that sounds most natural. The same advice therefore holds good for microphonic work as for public singing. Free play of mind and muscle, and let your song float on the ether like a bird on the wing.

It might be useful to singers to point out that the making of gramophone records is in many ways a less onerous task today than in the acoustical recording days and also in the early years of electrical recording. Recordings nowadays are taken on tape and if mistakes are made, musical or technical, the machine can be stopped and restarted; in fact, the recording can be made by instalments and this is frequently the method adopted. Films are made by instalments and all the perfected "shots" put together by the technicians. Sound recordings are now made in the same way.

Years ago recordings were made on a wax disc and if mistakes or accidents occurred the recording had to be restarted *from the beginning* and the performer had to keep on until a perfect *complete recording* had been made. The job required tremendous concentration, nerves of steel and a not inconsiderable measure of good luck. Just imagine for one moment the strain on the nerves in making a record of "The Lord Chancellor's Song" Act II, *Iolanthe*, commonly known as "The Nightmare Song". Four-and-a-quarter minutes of non-stop patter;

one slip and it had to start all over again. A nightmare indeed! I have done it and I know. Nowadays the song can be recorded in bits and the back-room boys do the knitting.

The conditions for artists in the recording studios have been greatly eased. Caruso, Battistini, McCormack, Chaliapin, Tetrazzini, Harry Lauder, Harry Fragson, George Robey and other great performers had to make records under the old conditions; but I wonder whether the improved technical operations have resulted in the discovery of greater artists than those I have mentioned. I reserve to myself the right to express honest doubts. This may be an irrelevant observation but—it is a thought.

The introduction and the development of stereophonic recording has not added to the trials and tribulations of the singers; indeed, they have been relieved of much personal responsibility. What is required of them is a good job of work as singers and performers; the technical staff will take care of the rest of the operations. What the latter cannot do is to turn a bad performance into a good one. So, in the end, it adds up to this: the primary responsibility for the making of a good record, mono or stereo, is the artist's. Any artist worthy of that description gladly accepts his or her responsibilities.

The subject of crooning has no place in a book on singing, because crooning is not legitimate singing as ordinary musical people understand the word. Nevertheless, there are dozens, if not hundreds, of radio singers of "pop" songs who earn handsome sums of money warbling over the air to the delight of a huge audience of listeners. Obviously they must have something to enable them to capture the ears of the public to the almost hysterical extent they do. They have "a something" in a large measure. They have the knack of pouring out emotion with uninhibited frankness; they can create an aura of sincerity, sometimes difficult for intelligent people to swallow; their articulation is always crystal clear, even if their pronunciation of words is distorted; they have an intriguing trick of breaking the rhythm by sliding and slurring over the bar lines and then straightening out the rhythmic flow of the melody in their own saccharine way. To quote W. S. Gilbert, "It is purely a matter

F

of skill, Which all may attain if they will". It is a skill that no genuine singer need bother to attain.

A technical description of the pop singer's method is well-nigh impossible; the approximation to a description would be to say that they sing all the time on the soft palate; as it were, on the back of the throat and at half-voice. But as the majority of them are only half-voiced anyway they make the microphone supply the volume of tone they cannot produce themselves. It really is fake singing and the resultant treacly sound acts like an opiate on an audience that wants nothing better than to swim dreamily in sentimental musical and lyrical ooze. This sort of singing and the music that goes with it has enriched song-writers, song publishers and pop singers alike, just as the sale of tranquillizers has enriched the manufacturers of drugs.

A healthy singer should steer clear of drugs especially if he or she wishes to make a successful career, so let us pass on to examine the prospects of singing as a career.

IX

SINGING AS A CAREER

ALTHOUGH it is probably unnecessary to do so, I think it advisable to state quite clearly that the title of this chapter is addressed specifically to the solo singer.

The desire to be alone is not a normal instinct in human nature; humanity, particularly the male half of it, is actuated very largely by the herd instinct, and hermits are few and far between. It is to be observed also that those who *do* seek the contemplative life usually find it in monastic communities where men (or women) can be alone, together.

On the other hand, the desire to sing, dance, act, perform, alone —that is, solo—is a primeval instinct deeply embedded in the whole of the human race.|The moment a child has learned to stand and put one foot in front of another, to say a word, or even a syllable, its first instinct is to give a solo performance of its newly-acquired skill, and in spite of the initial disasters and disappointments it will persevere towards complete mastery with a tenacity that in adults would be terrifying. Later on, as the emotional nature and the mental capacity of the child develops, various complexes arise giving birth to a number of checking actions that might be generalized in the one word "inhibitions", or more colloquially, "shynesses". It is not my purpose here to attempt to trace or explain the curious workings that take place in the hidden recesses of the human brain and their effect upon our emotional natures and upon human action and inaction. Let us accept the fact, for it is a fact, that as our individual natures evolve and develop, the desire to indulge in solo performances grows increasingly less, except in the case of a small minority who still retain the childlike uninhibited and unselfconscious desire to express, in voice and movement, songs and stories either heard, learned or imagined. This small minority of people who possess a natural instinct for singing and acting is still further reduced during the course of acquiring the necessary technique and education to enable the embryo artists to co-ordinate and develop their natural gifts. So eventually the number of people who continue to pursue the idea of becoming solo-performers dwindles to a comparatively small percentage of the population; the rest—and here I refer particularly to singers—content themselves and satisfy their musical needs by singing in groups or choirs; how well they do that in Great Britain all the world knows.

Singing has been encouraged from the earliest times by all the races of the world that have attained a degree of cultured and ordered way of life. The Greeks, significant and far-reaching as were their contributions to the history of the drama and mime, do not seem to have developed the art of singing in the theatre and public demonstrations beyond that of the chorus. Doubtless they had chorus leaders who might be described as soloists, but not such as would measure up to our modern ideas of solo singers. St. Sylvester, Pope of Rome A.D. 314 to 335, is generally accepted as being the founder of the first official school of song. Music had now begun to play an integral part in the offices of the church, and the necessity for trained bodies of singers became more and more pressing. It is from the first singing school in Rome and others that followed, most of them under the auspices of the Church, that the science and art of solo-singing traces its birth.

What I have already set down by way of historical notes is sketchy, but this book does not pretend to be a history of singing. However, enough has been said to show and to prove that the art of, and systematized instruction in, singing dates back to the fourth century; a cultural heritage which makes all true devotees of the art justly proud. Let us now think back to the state of musical affairs as they affected the solo singer thirty years ago.

Western music is today dominated by the composer. There was a time, however, when the composer and performer were one; indeed, when the composer was the servant of the performer. That relationship has gone for ever. Therefore in glancing back thirty years, and in order to adjust our sense of perspective, it would be useful if we passed in review the names of a few composers whose actual achievements in 1933 had justly established their reputations.

Richard Strauss was 69, Vaughan Williams 61, John Ireland 54, Igor Stravinsky 51, Sir Arthur Bliss 42, Darius Milhaud 41, Paul Hindemith 38, Francis Poulenc 34, Aaron Copland 33, Sir William Walton 31, Samuel Barber 23, Benjamin Britten 20. Britten is rightly included in this list because from the start of his career he was known to other and older composers as a boy wonder. In their various ways and styles all these composers made important contributions to the national library of vocal music; at any rate, contributions important enough to find places in the standard repertoire— that is, a repertoire with which all worth-while singers should have a more than passing acquaintance. Are the leading composers of our own day making equally valuable contributions? History alone can give the final answer to this very difficult question; it must content us for the present to record that contemporary opinion says—No.

Music has changed its pattern during the last thirty years and now addresses itself in a new form of language, rather less to the emotions than it does to the intellect. Modern composers—particularly the Serial ones—ask little from singers in the way of clean-cut, melodic line drawing and good tone production.

The professional singer's repertoire thirty years ago consisted of the standard oratorios, operas, *lieder* and ballads; music that called for technique and a real voice for its performance and its acceptance by the public. The same repertoire is required from the singer of today and the same ability to perform it, because the general public, whose interest and approbation provide the solo singer with his means of livelihood, not only wants to understand music but also wants to enjoy it. To the standard repertoire must be added a knowledge of the vocal music of the modern school that requires less preoccupation with pure sound and more attention to mechanical accuracy and the subservience of the personal equation. In other words, the demands made upon the solo singer have increased. Unlike the singers of old he is no longer a dictator—he is now the servant of both public and composer. The former demands entertainment and enjoyment; the latter, industry and obedience. The men who will see to it that industry and especially obedience are forthcoming are the conductors, the pampered matadors of the musical arena. The gladiatorial operatic days of Chaliapin and Caruso have passed away. The operatic gladiators of our day direct operations from the orchestral pit and we are invited to hear Rudolfo So-and-So's *Otello*, not the gentleman you will see and hear on the stage. It is a brave new world and bravery will be required to face it.

At this point I must make an attempt to answer the various questions that inevitably spring to the mind of anyone who has serious thoughts about becoming a professional singer. "What are the qualities and qualifications necessary for success?" I cannot answer the question in that form, because success is an elusive thing and has often been captured by the least worthy people. Let us put the question in another way. "What are the qualities and qualifications necessary to become a solo singer and to *deserve* success?" To become a singer it is first of all necessary to have a voice. This seemingly obvious reply at once raises an argument. What is a voice? The replies are many and widely different. I have already given my definition in Chapter I.

If success is the goal we wish to keep before our eyes then let us hope we have, or can acquire, the power to develop the personality God has given to us.

The task of learning to sing well, with its four or maybe five essentials, is not impossible; it can be achieved by normal young men and women who, possessing reasonably good voices and a taste and feeling for art, have the earnest desire, the intelligence, the industry and the patience to learn how to sing.

I use the word "intelligence" advisedly. Most normal men and women possess intelligence but it requires to be developed, and this brings me to the question, "What general standard of education is required?"

When solo singers have mastered the technique of their art, it is their high calling, their privilege, to use their skill to bring to mankind the message and the dreams of the poets and the music-makers. To do this they should have a knowledge and a love of literature and poetry. They should be able to appreciate the vocal flavour of words and make them not only mean what they say but sound what they mean.

We all know of instances of singers who had little or no education but who climbed to stardom simply and solely through the glory and beauty of their voices. That day has passed and gone, never to return. The programme of work to be carried out by the busy singer of our own time is a formidable one, requiring musicianship, quickness of perception, the actor's gift for characterization and the power to absorb the music and afterwards transmit it with the sincerity of a well-balanced mind. To sum up, the minimum standard of education required is Secondary or Grammar School plus specialization in music and literature.

The technical training required to become a well-equipped singer, its approximate cost and where it can be obtained make a tripartite question of special importance. I have already stated what I believe to be the four or five most important things in the art of singing. To learn them, master them, weld them and then use the new-found skill in performance with facility and ease will require at least four years' continuous and intensive study. Few people imagine that cricket or football can be learned in five minutes, therefore I find it difficult to understand why some of them hope to become reasonably good singers in half a dozen lessons. The Italian singers of the old school (and their British contemporaries) were expected to put in five years of hard work at fundamentals, and they were not expected to make any public appearances during that time. That a singer or two here and there did make an occasional appearance is true, but those appearances were few and far between. Today there is a tendency to streamline and speed up the period of training. Indeed, it is possible for the possessor of a rather more than good natural voice to leap into notoriety (not fame) after the briefest acquaintance with the tenets of the art of singing and only a nodding acquaintance with the art of music.

What is the result? After floundering about for two or three years in the land of the limelight without either map or compass, it becomes obvious that the voices are wearing out through the lack of a basic technique, and the sad end of it all is that they are compelled to retire to that obscurity from which they never should have emerged.

The moral of it all is, if you wish to become a singer who can stay the course, don't rush your training; make up your mind to a minimum period of four years. What will it cost and where can one obtain it? The fees at our principal schools of music are in the region of £135 a year. Private tuition is, as a rule, more expensive, some teachers charging a fixed rate per lesson and others making, in effect, a slight reduction by charging a fixed rate per term of x lessons. A familiar example of the latter custom is twelve lessons for the price of ten. The cost of private tuition must obviously be a matter for negotiation between teacher and pupil, but it is only fair to point out that the financial side of private tuition is governed to some extent by the law of supply and demand.

Teachers who are distinguished, famous or merely fashionable can command their own price, but in practice the best teachers, however famous, rarely make extortionate demands. The question of where tuition can be obtained is a very difficult one to answer. Honesty compels me to say that there are very few people who really have the knowledge, the experience and the flair for teaching singing. Our leading schools of music can offer the student the services of qualified teachers, and generally speaking one is safe in their hands, but it would be foolish to assert that one teacher is as good as another.

I think it only right to point out that several famous teachers in private practice also hold professorships at our schools of music. The question is a very delicate one and I must leave it, uttering these warnings as I do so. Don't assume that because a teacher's name is well known he or she is necessarily competent; nor must it be assumed that because a singer has had a distinguished public career he or she will automatically repeat their success in the field of teaching. In fact, don't assume anything. The reputation of a teacher must stand or fall by the success of his pupils; not the accidental success, but the solid success and the ability to stand up to the storm of a busy and long working life. Some racing stables have a reputation for producing winners of classic races; other stables, to put the matter both mildly and kindly, are not so fortunate. The reader will ponder this parable.

Before embarking upon any professional career it is not unusual for the young aspirant to make some enquiries about the amount of income it is possible to earn. Many professions have fixed minima for those who are fully qualified, but the profession of a solo performer is not one of them. When one comes to think about the matter this is not surprising because, in order to be a solicitor, physician, surgeon, chartered accountant, architect, chemist, schoolmaster and so on, a definite course of study has to be undertaken, costing in some cases a considerable sum of money, and students are not allowed to practise in their chosen profession until they have satisfied a responsible board of examiners that they are fitted to do so. The solo singer, on the other hand, is free to grow rich, or starve, according to the whim of a capricious board of examiners from whose decision there is no appeal: I refer, of course, to the public. Fundamentally true though this somewhat emphatic statement of mine is, strangely enough it is not the whole truth, because it sweeps out of consideration many factors that shape the destinies of a number of singers who, not being potential "stars", are accepted by the public in a casual sort of way. This type of singer often succeeds in making a prosperous living through musicianship, reliability, industry and the gift of being able to get on with people. They form a large bloc of the singing profession, and it is not to the public and the impresarios that they look for support. They bid for the favour of the critics, conductors of choral societies, composers, secretaries of music clubs and the leaders of all those societies and coteries whose chief concern is the type or the novelty of the music to be presented rather than the quality of its performance. This is neither a bad nor a good thing. It is well known that some magnificent singers (magnificent in the purely vocal sense, I mean) are poor musicians and have neither the taste nor the desire to spend time learning new music that is unlikely to bring them sufficiently large financial returns. The potential "stars"—that is, those who have something special to offer in the way of quality and size of voice plus technique, personality and showmanship—have little to worry about; such worries as they have are taken off their shoulders by the impresario and the agent who regard these gifted mortals as business propositions.

Lest the picture becomes too glittering, let me remind you that potential "stars" are very rare birds and that even the most attractive and persuasive publicity of the impresario and the agent cannot confer stardom upon them. This is done, if done at all, by the public, who elects its own favourites without help from or discussion with the professorial section of society. It will be seen, therefore, that my reference to the fairly large body of singers who never will be stars was in no sense derogatory; it was intended to bring a message of hope to all those singers who, having a love for music, are prepared to carry out the usual professional commitments, spectacular and unspectacular, with all the skill at their command and with artistic integrity.

And now let me extend a message of hope to a smaller but certainly fairly prosperous body of singers who are never mentioned when solo singing is being discussed. I am speaking of those busy people who during the winter sing at popular concerts and all those social functions where the stress is laid upon the entertainment value rather than upon the music. In the summer they sing in concert parties and summer shows at holiday resorts, and the financial result of the year's hard work, for they have to work hard, is often sufficiently rewarding to hold in thrall a few singers whose natural abilities would admit them to more artistic spheres. It is interesting to reflect that in Great Britain some of our embryo stars have been drawn from this class of singer.

The explanation is, of course, simple. In order to be successful in the popular and smoking-concert world one must possess a voice that is pleasant to listen to and be able to present and interpret a song in an attractive way. With this comparatively elementary equipment it is possible for the singers with sufficient education and ambition to find a place for themselves in the ranks of the serious concert singers who might playfully but not unfittingly be described in the language of cricket as the recognized "county players".

I have talked of stars, serious singers (and oh, how dreadfully serious some of them are!) and smoking-concert singers, and hinted that the stars, whose business is managed by impresarios or agents, make handsome incomes, and that the majority of the members of the other two classes are prosperous. You may ask, "What do you mean by 'prosperous'?" The dictionary definition of the word is "thriving, flourishing, successful". I do not think it is possible to translate these glowing words into the language of finance and mean the same thing to all men. Prosperity in the modest professional sense means a thousand pounds a year and upwards. The singer and the actor are in a class apart inasmuch as they are not only one-man businesses but, unlike most other one-man businesses, they cannot employ anyone to carry on their work for them during periods of sickness, and when the time comes for them to retire they have no goodwill to sell. It is therefore necessary for the solo singer to put a higher financial value and meaning upon the word "prosperous" than the members of other professions who hold official appointments carrying pensions, or whose businesses are saleable and have market values, variable though they may be.

Furthermore, it must not be forgotten that a concert singer's fee is an inclusive one; so if, for instance, his gross turnover for the year is £1500 his net earnings will be considerably less. Here is an example of what happens to a fee during its transition from gross to net. A good, reliable artist living in London is engaged by an agent to sing, say, at Liverpool, for a fee of thirty guineas, i.e., £31 10s. 0d. Now watch what happens to the fee:

	£	s.	d.
Fee	31	10	0
Less 10% commission to the Agent	3	3	0
	28	7	0
Train fare—Second-class return	4	17	0
	23	10	0
Hotel	2	10	0
	21	0	0
Taxi, tips and *one* meal on train	1	10	0
	£19	10	0

NOTE: Train fares continue to rise.

Many well-known artists receive much higher fees and many more receive lower—I merely quote thirty guineas as an average figure, and my deductions for necessary expenses are based on a *very* modest estimate.

To return to the question, "What sort of income can be made as a solo singer?" I fear it is not possible to give a precise answer. It is useless to ask the artists themselves because those who *do* talk about their fees and their incomes always exaggerate. The incomes of singers who are regarded as "bookable", that is, "average", "good" and "very good" and all fairly well known, vary from £1000 to £2500 a year. A comparative handful are in the £3000-plus a year class. This range of attainable incomes compares very favourably with the financial rewards offered to university professors—see the advertisements in *The Times*. Indeed, a singer's career might make managers of football clubs green with envy. A soccer manager's job seems to be one of such total insecurity that I wonder anyone can ever be persuaded to take it on. Maybe, like singers, they love their work and are prepared to take any risks.

Leaving the subject of money, let us turn to a question that is closely related to the previous one, and one that exercises the minds of all who are just starting on the road. "How does one secure employment?" Or the more usual form of the question, "How does one get engagements?" I have been asked this question so often that I ought by now to have found a cast-iron reply. Alas! I have not.

When students complete their training, either at an academy, college or conservatoire or with a private tutor, they can, if they have won the confidence of their directors or teachers, obtain recommendations to agents, conductors, opera companies, the B.B.C., influential friends, and so on. The more usual method is for the students themselves to write to all likely sources of employment, mentioning their musical background both personal and practical, the personal part as a recommendation and the practical part as a kind of guarantee of musical fitness.

The letters, of course, take the form of asking for auditions, and it is at this point that our tribulations begin. A few lucky ones may get off to a flying start but I'm afraid the large majority have to tread a fairly long road of disappointment. It is one thing to ask for an audition and quite another to get one. It is not that employers or people who direct musical activities are hardhearted, indifferent, lazy or just plain stupid—not at all! The agents may have heard all the singers they can possibly cope with for the moment. If you are a bona fide professional the B.B.C. will certainly hear you sing, but you may have to wait a little while for an audition.

A few years ago the waiting list was so long that applicants had sometimes to wait for six months or more for an audition. At the time of going to press the situation is much easier; artists seldom have to wait longer than a month once their professional credentials have been accepted by the Controller of Music or his Deputy. Singers, and probably others of my readers, may be interested to know how the B.B.C. auditions are arranged and carried out.

First the applicant, having written to the B.B.C., will be sent a standard form. On this he must supply the information necessary to establish his professional status—a résumé of his experience as a public performer, backed up by details of at least three concert, oratorio or operatic programmes of recent date in which he has sung. (Obviously, copies of genuine Press criticisms, preferably quoted in their entirety, would be welcomed.) Charity concerts and such-like affairs should not be included. Then, if the B.B.C. officials are satisfied that he is really a professional singer of some attainment, his name will be added to the list of artists agreed to be heard.

The auditions always take place in the afternoon, either in the Concert Hall at Broadcasting House or at one of the studios in Delaware Road, Maida Vale. Fifteen minutes are allowed for each singer, with an actual *singing time* of twelve-and-a-half minutes. The first audition is a "Preliminary" and if the auditionee is successful he or she will soon be offered a final audition. Very occasionally an artist gives a performance of such outstanding excellence at the first hearing, that the formality of a "Final" is dispensed with.

May I respectfully offer a word of advice on the delicate question of accompanists? It is natural that a young singer (or instrumentalist, for that matter) should believe he will have more confidence when facing the microphone if he brings along his regular accompanist. If that accompanist is first class, and accustomed to the conditions and acoustics of broadcasting studios, well and good. But so often the visiting accompanist is as inexperienced in broadcasting as the singer, and in consequence just as nervous. I do not ignore the obvious advantages of having rehearsed the audition programme beforehand. But I would emphasise to the apprehensive auditionee that the Corporation always has at hand an excellent accompanist, familiar with a vast repertoire, upon whom he may rely utterly not only for musical support but also for a sympathetic understanding of his nervousness. The official in charge—usually a charming hostess—will always grant a few extra minutes for quick consultation with the accompanist and even for a short trial run of a page or two.

The panel of judges at these auditions consists of three or four people of whom certainly one, and very often two, will be outside assessors, i.e., experienced professionals who are not on the B.B.C.'s permanent staff. The artists are heard over a loudspeaker in a room that is entirely screened off from the audition studio. The panel is not given any information about the candidates, nor can they see them; all that is typed on their Report Sheet is this: No. 1—Tenor; No. 2—Soprano, and so on. Each judge writes an independent report, without consultation with his colleagues. Discussion among them during auditions is in fact strongly discouraged. The reports are collected and a few days later discussed in confidence by a specialist committee. Having served on these panels from time to time as an outside assessor, I can vouch for the scrupulous fairness of the conduct of these proceedings. I know of no other organization which goes to such trouble and expense over this important matter: certainly no theatre either could or would, if only for economic reasons.

Opera companies may have completed their contractual arrangements for the season and although the influential musical friends may readily hear the youngsters sing, it is not always possible for them to hold out a helping hand with the promptitude the suppliant had hoped for. The short period—I hope it is a short one—when the young singer first sets out to find work and seems to meet rebuffs and empty promises on every hand is a time of trial, both of patience and character.

A sense of humour will help at this time; and with this gift plus both patience and courage he or she will be the better fitted to fight the real battle that lies ahead. "Yes," you may say, "that's all very well, but this battle that lies ahead will have to take care of itself—I'm asking how one gets engagements *now*." The cold but true answer is this: Hope and pray that someone will give you an engagement (yes—without fee, if that is the only way one can be got) and, having sampled the goods you have to offer, is sufficiently satisfied to induce him to offer you a re-booking, and maybe recommend you to someone else who can also offer you an engagement.

If you really have the goods to offer and present them as an artist should, with sincerity, the news will soon spread and presently you will begin to realize that at last you have got your feet on the first rung of the ladder and must now begin to climb.

You may never reach the top, but if you are made of the stuff professionals are made of, and need to be made of, you can have a lot of fun during the climb. The gift of laughter will help a great deal and ease the strain of all the pushing and shoving that takes place on the rather overcrowded ladder that leads to fame and fortune. It would seem that another question is pressing its way forward, demanding a reply. "Is the profession (the solo performer's section of it) overcrowded?" The ready answer is—Yes. It always has been overcrowded; by that I mean there is not enough work to provide the struggling mass of competitors with a reasonable living income. The *best* singers do not have to compete with each other to get work; the *work* competes for *them*. In other words, the good singers, the singers who have won the confidence of the public and the music organizers alike cannot accept all the work that is offered to them. On the other hand, there is a pretty fierce scramble for the crumbs that fall from the busy singers' tables, and I fear that many of the weaker ones (weaker in the professional sense) are trodden underfoot. This is not the law of the jungle as some squeamish people may think; it is the law of common sense, rough though it may be in application.

The late Sir Landon Ronald once said to me, "Baker, if you want someone to do a job, and do it well, always go to a busy person." How right he was; artists are busy because they can be relied upon to do good, acceptable work.

After all has been said, no one is compelled to be a solo singer. We choose this exciting, adventurous but precarious calling of our own free will, and if after offering our services to the public in the open market we find there are not enough buyers to make the game worth the candle, we shall then have to face one of two inexorable alternatives—retire gracefully or be starved out. If this seems unsympathetic and unduly forthright, I apologize, at the same time asking my readers not to lose heart but to reflect upon and to take comfort from the fact that they themselves applaud the moral law that governs all sport: "Let the best man win."

I do not know how many people in the United Kingdom are occupied with the problem of making a living as a solo singer, but there are upwards of four hundred solo singers on the register of the Incorporated Society of Musicians. We must add to this figure a conjectural number of those who are not members of the corporate body to which I have referred, and who function as soloists, not in the regular concert world but in the theatre, in vaudeville, and also on the lighter side of musical entertainment. Anyhow, whatever figure we arrive at, and I think it will be a large one, we can say the profession is overcrowded but there is always room and need for recruits, not only to make up the slack caused by those who fall by the way but to supply the new blood that is so necessary to keep the profession alive. Go ahead, young people, the world is yours to conquer.

Whether the modern world will extend a very hearty welcome to would-be conquerors is another matter, but those who belong to the present generation will know best how to cope with the situation. One can strive against all kinds of adversity—ill-health, lack of a cultural and sympathetic home-life in one's early years, lack of spiritual teaching, lack of self-discipline, the ill-effects of under-nourishment and the ill-effects of self-indulgence; one can strive against all these handicaps and win; in that sense one can claim to have conquered something.

If you have not conquered the world you will at least have

G

become, to a rather greater than less degree, a master of yourself, and that is a conquest of which few mortals are capable.

The path trodden by the musical adventurers of the present day is a less rugged one than that trodden by the bold, gay hopefuls of thirty years ago. Today there are scholarships, exhibitions, prizes, grants from County Councils—all sorts of "bits and pieces" handed out to deserving students to help them on the way to becoming self-supporting professionals.

The amelioration of the normal lot of the student by the Government (National, County, Urban, Rural) through many official channels and subsidized and sponsored Councils is a good thing in many ways, in that it provides opportunities and relieves those who are able to grasp them of unnecessary worry. Whether the easier conditions will lead to the discovery and development of singers comparable to the great ones of the golden age of song is extremely doubtful. However, since modern social thinking and planning frowns on individual greatness in any walk of life, it may be that in aiming at producing good, musically solid, technically efficient and hard-working solo singers we are creating a type that will fit more cleanly and comfortably into the world of music, dominated as it is by the conductor and the composer to a greater extent than at any time throughout its history.

The nation, through the Government, is sponsoring and subsidizing the performance of music both directly and indirectly, but the indirect method is the one usually adopted.

The B.B.C. is, of course, the biggest supplier of music in Great Britain, and although it is a self-governing body its Governors are appointed by the Government and the Corporation carries on its work under a charter granted to it for a definite term of years by Parliament.

The Arts Council draws its funds from H.M. Treasury, and gives financial aid in the form of subsidies to very many musical organizations, great and small, from opera houses and the great orchestras down to lowly but gallant music clubs in obscure towns. It does noble work.

The British Council exports British culture in all its forms and, like the Arts Council, draws its funds from the Treasury.

My reason for mentioning these public bodies as agents of the Government is to draw attention to the ever-growing tendency towards centralized control. Years ago singers were a very independent lot; the attitude they adopted in their professional affairs was, "Well, if you don't like me there are other people who do," and, "That's my fee, take it or leave it; if *you* won't pay it there are plenty of others who will." It was a comfortable and carefree way of approaching life.

Today, if a singer quarrels with a client he may, for all he knows, be quarrelling, in effect, with a syndicate of clients. These new governing bodies, idealistic and benevolent though they are in spirit and intention, are managed by human beings, and human beings have their likes and dislikes; some, more dangerous, enjoy the use of power and authority.

It is easy to realize therefore that the old attitude of "an artist is free and independent and other artists' affairs are no concern of mine", coupled with the dog-fight competition of every man for himself, is definitely a thing of the past. Today the solo performers cannot live in splendid isolation, they must join their confrères in protecting the acknowledged rights and customs of their profession, and in furthering the interests of the profession as a whole in a social and economic world that is evolving at top speed.

The Incorporated Society of Musicians is the only organization that can meet and take care of the needs of a solo singer. It is not a trade union; I suppose it could be described as a protective society, on the lines of the B.M.A. and the Law Society, but unfortunately lacking the influence of those two politically powerful associations.

Should the solo singer's activities drift, either by chance or design, towards the operatic field and theatre work generally, it will be necessary for him or her to join British Actors' Equity. This is a trade union, and has the support of the leading personalities of the theatrical profession, all of whom are members.

In the process of writing this chapter I have endeavoured, in a

G*

succinct and direct way, to answer the sort of questions put to me on countless occasions during my lengthy career by earnest and sincere young people who were trying to make up their minds and gather sufficient courage to start out on the great adventure of offering themselves and their songs to the public. However, since social and working conditions not only in one particular profession but in all forms of employment are subject to rapid changes in an evolutionary world, I am acutely aware that some of my replies may soon become out-of-date. It will be for the young singers to watch all the moves, the changes and the adjustments in conditions for themselves.

There is another question, and one that I must confess I face with some feelings of trepidation—"What books can be profitably studied?" This question obviously implies the reading of books that will be useful to one in one's day-to-day work.

There are a number of books that young singers should "read, mark, learn and inwardly digest." Unfortunately the large majority of our singers are not bookishly inclined. They will work hard at their singing; indeed, in the north-countryman's expression, they will "sing till the cows come home", but reading is not their strong suit. There are exceptions, and brilliant exceptions, too, but eighty per cent of our songsters prefer to sing rather than read their way through life. For the most part they are simple-hearted folk, and provided that they can be reasonably sure that when they call out "I have a song to sing O" the crowd will respond readily and cheerfully, "Sing me your song O", they are happy.

If I can persuade the singers to glance at a book or two, here are my suggestions:

BACHNER, LOUIS, *Dynamic Singing*, Dennis Dobson. This is an excellent book; I cannot recommend it too highly.

DAVIES, FFRANGCON, *The Singing of the Future*, John Lane. This should be read, re-read and browsed over time and time again throughout one's career. There are some characteristic overstatements in the book, but on the whole it contains more truth about the art, the technique, the practice and the very purpose of singing, than any book of its kind in existence.

MOORE, GERALD, *The Unashamed Accompanist*, Ascherberg. Singers may ask why I recommend this book. Because accompanists of Gerald Moore's artistic stature know all about the singers, with their tricks, foibles and inaccuracies. The good accompanist is like the wise Father Confessor; he knows most things and is never surprised, but with the broad sympathy that characterizes both self-effacing priests, *musica et ecclesia*, he can teach us a lot, if we are but humble enough to learn.

PLUNKET GREENE, H., *Interpretation in Song*, Macmillan. Every singer should possess this book. There is not much about technique in it, and with much of what there is, I disagree. However, on the subject of song interpretation my friend, the late Harry Plunket Greene, was an authority worth listening to. If you really wish to learn, study this book with care; it is written by one who was a scholar, a musician and a good performer.

Read all the musical biographies you can get hold of; the auto-biographies are often funnier but not so instructive.

The questions (self-posed, I admit, but typical ones) having been answered, I think it is now time to look around us in a general way before finally wishing the welcome recruits to the noble army of songsters Good Luck!

I embraced the career of a professional singer—that means, a solo singer—in 1908, and in spite of all the slings and arrows of a not too outrageous fortune I can look back upon my professional life and say at once, and honestly, that it has been a happy one. If you are nursing the idea that by becoming a professional singer you stand a good chance of making money—real money, I mean—throw the idea away at once. The number of singers throughout the world who can make large incomes is point something per cent; but on the other hand, it is quite possible to become modestly prosperous, and what is more important, lead a happy life.

Prosperity and happiness are not necessarily marriageable terms, but it is noticeable that they often live very near to each other. Happiness is a state of mind and a disposition of the heart. Matter-of-fact people say it is largely a state of health. I will accept this, reserving to myself the right to observe that I have known some healthy miseries in my time. Let us say, then, that happiness is an amalgam of the mental, the emotional and the chemical states of the body. The question at once arises, "What sort of happiness?" Is it the bland happiness of a healthy and contented animal, or is it the controlled, mentally-balanced happiness of a human being, the species endowed by God with the unique gift of art? If it is the latter, and I believe this to be true, our happiness will be born of a mental desire to do good work, the best we can give, and to offer that work with a free heart to the people.

The public's emotional reaction to a gift beautifully fashioned and so freely given is immediate and atomic in its power. You will be acclaimed, and with the acclamation will come the prosperity we shall hope you have deserved.

No! Prosperity and happiness are not interchangeable terms, but together they can produce the contented and successful artist.

Do be persuaded by one who has been a solo singer for fifty-five years and a professional musician for sixty years that the only way to be reasonably sure of making a successful career is to possess an instrument, i.e., a voice that is in tune, that can be heard and that is fit to listen to and worthy of the best that is in music. Remember that music is not a game of chance, it is an art; therefore, study it. Don't forget that through the medium of song it is your privilege, as I have said before, to bring the messages and the stories of the poets to mankind, so let your powers of articulation be guided by intelligence.

Finally, a singer's life is a hard one and you cannot, try as you will, escape from the work that it entails.

To sum up, in order to be reasonably sure of success you must:

(1) Possess a good voice
(2) Be a musician
(3) Use intelligence
(4) Work

"Beginners, please!" (says the voice of the call boy)—The stage awaits you. Good luck—and enjoy yourselves.

EPILOGUE

THIS book has dealt chiefly with the main activities of a singer's life, which consist of oratorio, opera, broadcasting, recording (if one can get such work) and a passing reference has been made to what one could aptly call bread-and-butter concerts—never to be despised.

But there are opportunities for work at Music Clubs, where one is expected to present a recital programme of *lieder* and/or art songs. The subject of *lieder* singing is a complex one and very few, even of the generally-accepted *lieder* singers, measure up entirely to a standard of perfection. On the one hand there are singers with beautiful voices and obvious technical skill who often seem strangely at sea in poems that seek to express subtle and abstract ideas or emotional half-lights. On the other hand, there are singers whose cultural and mental equipment fit them to tackle almost anything in the field of art-songs but whose lack of technical skill in voice production prevents them from implementing their artistic intentions. I say, therefore, that to sing art-songs one requires a perfected technique (this point cannot be stressed too hard) a cultured mind, an innate sense of poetry, deep musical feeling and absolute truth of expression. In short, the complete equipment of the master-singer must be brought to bear on this, the most delightful branch of a singer's work.

I put technique as the first requirement because, however cultured a man may be or however deep his emotional feelings, he cannot find full expression unless his voice responds unconsciously and automatically to his will. The voice is the singer's instrument—let him be the master of it.

One of the troubles of the contemporary musical world is that singers who do not possess sufficiently good voices to tackle the classical and standard vocal repertoires or to sing simple ballad tunes attractively, try to make up their deficiencies as vocal artists by specializing, as they euphemistically describe it, in *lieder*, often in languages they cannot speak and do not understand. This is pure self-deception, and apart from being a trial of patience to the listening public, these inadequate performers bring the art of *lieder* singing into disrepute. All the renowned *lieder* singers graduated as "general practitioners", not as "specialists".

May I also remind you that the greatest singers and actors were not recruited from the ranks of "ladies and gentlemen"; therefore, to thine own self be true.

Finally, always remember these words, written by Gounod to his young composer friend, Georges Bizet: "No master, whoever he may be, can any more annihilate a personality than he can create one . . . Personality is the direct expression, the involuntary emanation, the inseparable physiognomy of a being; it is indelible."

· · · · · ·

"Since singing is so good a thing
I wish all men would learn to sing."

WILLIAM BYRD